D1133417

A Cart Full of
MAGIC

© Studio Republic

About the Author

Ileana Abrev had been a practicing witch for more than twenty years. Originally from Cuba, she now lives in Queensland, Australia. With knowledge passed down to her by her father, an esteemed Santero, Ileana guides her clients on a daily basis to solve problems while assisting them with spell casting for a positive outcome.

ILEANA ABREV

A Cart Full of

MAGIC

✓ HEALING POWERS

✓ HAPPINESS

✓ CONCENTRATION

✓ LOVE

✓ PROTECTION

✓ *Your Secret Supermarket Shopping List*

FIRST EDITION
First Printing, 2018

Book design by Bob Gaul
Cover design by Kevin R. Brown
Editing by Rosemary Wallner

Llewellyn Publications is a registered trademark of Llewellyn Worldwide Ltd.

Library of Congress Cataloging-in-Publication Data (Pending)
ISBN: 978-0-7387-5496-3

Llewellyn Worldwide Ltd. does not participate in, endorse, or have any authority or responsibility concerning private business transactions between our authors and the public.

All mail addressed to the author is forwarded, but the publisher cannot, unless specifically instructed by the author, give out an address or phone number.

Any Internet references contained in this work are current at publication time, but the publisher cannot guarantee that a specific location will continue to be maintained. Please refer to the publisher's website for links to authors' websites and other sources.

Llewellyn Publications
A Division of Llewellyn Worldwide Ltd.
2143 Wooddale Drive
Woodbury, MN 55125-2989
www.llewellyn.com

Printed in the United States of America

CONTENTS

PART ONE: From Everyday Products to Magical Items

1: Introduction   3

2: A Short History of Grocery Shopping   7

3: Magical Supplies and Tools   13

4: Not Everything Has a Magical Correlation   17

5: Visualization   19

6: Grocery Shopping with Intention   25

7: Using this Book   29

PART TWO: Food, Drink, and More

8: Vegetables   35

9: Fruits   51

10: Bread   65

11: Dairy   67

12: Nuts and Seeds   75

13: Grains and Legumes   85

14: Eggs   91

15: Sugar   95

16: Baking Goods   99

17: Honey   107

18: Vinegar   111

19: Oils   115

20: Salt   127

21: Herbs and Spices   133

22: Coffee and Tea   159

23: Water   165

24: Juice Drinks   171

25: Alcoholic Beverages   175

Part Three: Household, Hygiene, Beauty, and Other Items

26: Flowers   181

27: Essential Oils   197

28: Hygiene and Daily Ritual Products   219

29: Beauty   229

30: Housewares   241

31: Cleaning Products   255

32: Hardware   265

33: Seeds for Planting   273

34: Bird Food   277

35: Other Products   281

Part Four: Enhancing Magical Work

36: Applying Color in Magic   305

37: Allowing Outside Influences   333

38: Blending Energies 343

39: Cleansing Your Home Physically and
Spiritually 349

Reflections in Closing 355

Index 357

Chris

Our friendship has walked miles and forever will.

....

John

You are and forever will be my favorite Aussie.

Part One

FROM EVERYDAY PRODUCTS TO MAGICAL ITEMS

✓ HEALING POWERS

✓ HAPPINESS

✓ CONCENTRATION

✓ LOVE

✓ PROTECTION

INTRODUCTION

In today's world of online shopping, resources for magical supplies have grown so much since I first wrote *White Spells: Magic for Love, Money & Happiness*. You can buy just about anything online now, especially the resins and rare herbs for specific spells. But supplies to bring or vanish spiritual energy to manifest stability in your home are endless, and the supermarket is just another convenient place where you can shop for them.

In this book, I transform the supermarket into a magical place you never knew existed. Produce will come alive with its magical essence. A single nut will bring prosperity and wisdom into your world; a safety pin could be a quick means of protection. Together, we'll make shopping at your supermarket a fun and magical experience and improve your emotional well-being, finances, love, and spiritual health and happiness by imbuing the weekly expedition with a magical perspective.

I'm always trying to make things easier for those I help. Simplicity in magic is what makes our minds focus on the intent we wish to bring forth. I have found that the simpler something is, the more motivation we have to do it and this in turn brings a positive outcome.

Witches have a way of interpreting all that there is and what it could be. We make do with what we have. We conjure from the Earth. We respect what has been freely given with unconditional love. We do not take what is not ours. We respect other's faith, even if we cannot justify it, and understand that individuality is what makes us all unique and beautiful.

A Cart Full of Magic is about convenience and know-how for the modern-day witch. I hope to make you a little bit wiser and more aware of what you purchase, what items could mean or represent to you once you bring your groceries home, and the many ways your weekly supermarket expedition can be used to bring love, happiness, health, and protection into your home.

Once you bring home items from your secret supermarket shopping list, be a little more conscious of your magical purchases. Don't just display flowers; display them for a purpose, for love or happiness. Don't put a bunch of fresh basil straight in the fridge; display it in a vase for protection. Every time you eat a nut, feel protected and assured that all will be as it should be.

A SHORT HISTORY OF GROCERY SHOPPING

We have come a long way since those first early days when homegrown vegetables, fruits, herbs, and grains were shared or swapped between communities or farmers. Outdoor markets once were the only place to stock up for the winter and where witches gathered most of their precious supplies if they didn't grow them. Witches spent most winters creating potions to assist the sick, help those with their spiritual path, and aid with the many births they encountered. In those early times, salt was a very expensive commodity as it was an essential part of preserving meat, seafood, and dairy products in the absence of refrigeration. There were no pesticides, everything was more than organic, and if it wasn't in season, you didn't find it at the market until it was.

The food on the table identified one's financial status within the community, and sadly to this date it still does. More often than not, our ancestors ate the same meal for days on end. Grains such as wheat, rye, oats, and barley were their staple diet. These were boiled down into soups, ground into flour to make bread, and malted for alcoholic beverages. Legumes provided protein, as meat was only available on rare occasions.

The introduction of the country general store in the middle of the 1800s dramatically changed the way people purchased food. These stores were unique and friendly; they had very little lighting, long counters, high shelves, and rounded glass drawers and bins filled with all sorts of grains.

There was hardly anything prepacked; goods were mostly sold by weight and mainly situated behind the counter. While the storekeeper individually wrapped your order, social interaction was at its peak, not only with the store-keeper but also with those waiting to be served. Stocking up at the general store was the daily or weekly social event some people looked forward to while others shunned, not wanting their business to become public knowledge in the town.

Once weighed, the price of each item was jotted down on a small piece of paper or added up in the storekeeper's head. This process was tedious and time-consuming, as there was limited staff and customers simply had to wait their turn.

By the early 1900s, those little stores had evolved into larger businesses that added more staff, cash registers, self-service shelves where shoppers could pick out their own foods, and rows and rows of prepackaged goods.

Today's conglomerates can overpower the buyer with their different brands and colorful labels. Major food companies now pay substantial fees for their products to be at eye level on the shelf, leaving other brands out of sight on the very bottom or very top shelves. For the most part, there is no escaping the conglomerates that have become a part of our society over recent decades.

Having access to everything we need in one place is a convenience a lot of people cannot live without. Our daily schedules and financial needs draw us to it like a magnet. Supermarket shopping is now a rite of passage and will be for generations to come.

Although there are still stores with that personal uniqueness of how it once was, you may need to travel far and wide to find them, and more often than not they don't stock your everyday needs. If they do, the limited buying power of these smaller stores mean you will pay substantially more. These types of stores are trendy to visit on weekends but are usually not suited for our daily needs—but don't you wish they existed to take us back to the simplicity we once had!

Not so long ago and even now, shoppers could not find organic products on supermarket shelves. Consumers who wanted them for health reasons or personal preference had to look elsewhere. The conglomerates saw the growing demand, however, and now offer organic products of all types.

MAGICAL SUPPLIES
AND TOOLS

The tools used in witchcraft define us in more ways than one. No altar is the same as another. Each one expresses an individuality that is within each of us, hidden and only exposed to those we confide in and trust. We practice our faith distinctively from other witches, as witchcraft does not depict a strict curriculum that must be followed. Our practice honors the God and Goddess and the Sabbaths by respecting a faith that is as old as time.

When we talk about the tools of witchcraft, one of the first items that come to mind is the pentagram. Throughout history, this controversial five-pointed geometric star has had a symbolism to cultures around the world, and witchcraft is one of them. The pentagram has many functions, from banishing to evoking spirit to centering one's intent.

Other tools include ritual and working knives, and cauldrons for cooking and making potions. Then there is the wand to channel energy; a chalice, representing the Water element, for offering; a broom to cleanse a sacred space; a feather to represent the element of Air; stones and crystals for Earth; and candles for Fire.

Apart from the tools, there are also the supplies of witchcraft such as herbs, flowers, ribbons, and much more. These supplies move or maintain spiritual energy for protection, love, health, wealth, and happiness and for what I call the "Witch's Art of Placement."

The Witch's Art of Placement is when we place or carry a needed energy (supply) to cause an effect, such as having a bowl of oranges in a basket to keep the love flowing within your home, or displaying a bunch of flowers to beautify a space or thank spirit for watching over us. We can also carry a drawstring bag containing all those magical little spices or trinkets to bring a need or to keep the flow of positive energy around us.

Everything in our home has a magical potential, and as long as we are aware of that potential, we can keep the energy flowing by evoking intent. And that is why this book is not about spell casting but about keeping positive energy flowing. Our spiritual liveliness is vital to our existence and what makes us human. The energy that flows within each one of us, be it positive or negative, is what we build our homes on.

A good example of that intent is vacuuming. Most of us vacuum once a week. We try to avoid it like a bad spirit and it haunts us until we actually do it. Over the years, however, I have looked at vacuuming the house in a different light. I use vacuuming not only to pick up dirt but also to pick up what I call "negative dirt."

Negative dirt is what we bring home from those we like and from those we do not. Every day, we tread where our nemesis treads. By accidentally, and without awareness, re-treading their steps, we bring their energies into our sacred space. Although this is the last thing we want to do, it is easily fixed: Sprinkle your floor or carpet lightly with salt, vacuum it, and as you do, visualize the negative dirt you wish to vanish. Let the vacuum cleaner suck up the negative dirt and then throw it in the trash never to be seen again. Your home will thank you for it and you will be better for it in the end.

NOT EVERYTHING HAS A MAGICAL CORRELATION

Not everything in the supermarket has a magical meaning; it would be silly to suggest it does. The small percentage of items or produce that have magical properties do not contain preservatives; thus, items such as prepackaged cookies, chips, canned vegetables, and pasta sauces are not used in magic.

As you can appreciate, there is no magic in a can of soup that you heat in the microwave for two minutes; but if you make the soup from scratch, it takes a magical direction. Once you add the first fresh ingredients into your pot, you are automatically thinking of the results you want to manifest. This makes the soup a magical tool, especially if you make it for someone who is ill.

I am also aware that there are known magical practices that require animal flesh; however, I'm not versed in those practices apart from Santería's offerings of animal flesh to celebrate a deity where everyone participates in the feast. There are negative connotations when animal flesh is used in magic, but none of them bear any positive outcome to improve your life, surroundings, or those around you.

The products found in the cleaning, housewares, hardware, hygiene, and beauty aisles have their own special essence. Something as simple as lipstick or a hairbrush may have no magical meaning, but the essence they represent is the key to manifestation—as long as you are able to look past what is deemed as the norm.

5

VISUALIZATION

Before searching the aisles of your local supermarket for magical items to achieve your intentions, I need to stress the importance of visualization in magic. Without visualization, an action has no validity and you will have trouble connecting to the Universe.

Our brain controls and coordinates our mental and physical actions, but the mind is different and is our biggest asset. The mind is the hard drive of our reasoning and function center, and what makes us human. The mind gathers thoughts, gives control to our imagination, and stimulates recognition of emotions. It governs our actions and attitudes to bring fulfilment to our thoughts and to make us persevere with our goals and intentions. But for the mind to function and work, it needs a controller to manage the mammoth hard drive that gives us movement and cognition, and that controller is you.

Knowing how to work and steer your mind is like learning a new computer software program. Some find it extremely easy, while others find it so hard that they give up before they even start. Then there are those who try on a constant basis to learn, but get distracted, opening programs and never quitting them, always trying to find a way around them causing a total shutdown of the system.

This analogy is the same for our thoughts. Our mind is in a constant state of flux. Our thoughts run faster than a rabbit, constantly changing patterns from one thought to another, one problem to another, holding on to emotional problems and hurts, thinking of what it should have been or what it was supposed to be.

Then there is what one of my friends calls "option anxiety": when we allow ourselves to let in a plethora of options.

One or two life options are reasonably acceptable, but any more than that causes nothing but confusion.

This makes our mind go into overdrive to the point of not being able to choose a definite path. The quicker you change those thought patterns that have no place in visualization, and the clearer and more precise your intent is in your mind, the better your transmission to the Universe.

What we do know about the mind is that if it's set on a charted, structured path, we are more likely to succeed. What this tells us is that we need to plan ahead and stick to a path with one thought, one wish, one intent at a time. By keeping it simple and not letting daily stressors interfere, you'll have a clearer vision to interpret and manifest.

Using positive visualization to direct your thoughts for manifestation is out there for the taking. Just think of yourself as the director in a movie. You have total control of your actions. You set the scenes you want to create and see them unfold firsthand. Be the director of your own life. Make it happen. Remember, you are the one with the power and you alone are responsible for the ins and outs of your thoughts. It is up to you to apply them negatively or positively.

Some people find visualization difficult, while others have no problems with it. If you can't visualize, don't worry about it; you can get the same effect by feeling the intent with all your heart. When I immerse myself in the intent I want to bring forth, I can see the outcome. This is a very powerful tool, not only in magic but also with every goal or dream you wish to manifest.

Remember that the mind cannot tell if what you are visualizing is real unless you tell your mind it is or it isn't. So don't destroy its interpretation of your intent—just go with it. Let the subconscious be the child who believes in fairy tales. Let the conscious mind be the vessel to start designing your life with clarity and purpose by letting go of your conditioning and embracing the wholeness of what it could be.

When it is time to shop for magical items, visualize your intent from the time you enter the store to the time you return home. Your intent should always be positive, and acute to the point that you have already seen the outcome even before you start. In magic, it's not a matter of *if* but *when*.

GROCERY SHOPPING
WITH INTENTION

The layout of a supermarket is practically the same in all countries. There are numerous aisles and within each one are thousands of products neatly arranged and packaged. The outside aisles around the perimeter are full of fresh produce, cold cuts, poultry, beef, fish, fresh breads, freshly baked cakes, and biscuits.

The inner aisles can get confusing with products packaged in all sorts of shapes, colors, and sizes. From Weight Watchers I learned that if you stayed away from the inner aisles except for the cleaning and hygiene sections, the chances of losing weight were much greater, and staying away from the inner aisles goes for magic as well.

The best time of the day to visit a supermarket is first thing in the morning or when it opens. This way, you can avoid crowds of people and shop in a relatively peaceful and leisurely atmosphere.

Become familiar with your store and download the app for it, if they have one. Make a list of the items you need for your weekly shopping expedition and if you like, make another list for your magical items; it is okay to combine the two lists as well. If you need basil to make a delicious pasta sauce and also need it to manifest financial stability, there is no need to buy two bunches. Just use the basil for your financial intent first then use the rest for your sauce recipe.

This goes for any magical needs. Always use an item for magic first before you eat, cook with, or use it. Be respectful to spirit and it will endeavor to favor your needs.

When at the store, try to be in a reasonable frame of mind—remember, you are shopping for a particular item to manifest a need. The last thing you need to be is moody, tired, or angry as you select magical items. If you are, you can actually kill the energy you were trying to bring on in the first place.

Make shopping a pleasant experience, have fun and keep your mind set on why you are there in the first place. Gather your thoughts—you are close to manifesting your intent. This notion alone should activate your endorphins and get the juices flowing.

Be aware of your mindset and stay in the moment. You have the power within you to manifest anything you wish, and you alone can make it happen. Just being part of the now is the fulfilment of all that there is and what you want it to be. When you enter the produce section, breathe in all those wonderful energies, look at the colors all around you. Let the experience be absorbed into your etheric field to strengthen your thoughts and align your chakras. Think of it as if you've been given a stimulant, and as this energy travels through all your nerve endings, be assured you have just been recharged.

You are the magician, you have total control of your destiny and the dreams you wish to become a reality. Stay in tune, think positively of the energy you want to bring to your home or to those you love. Stay focused on your intent; make it a part of you knowing that your magical needs are just a shopping cart away.

USING THIS BOOK

This first part has been an introduction, a beginning, a way for you to see how setting your mindset and using magical items can manifest an intention. Parts Two and Three of this book take you step-by-step through your supermarket. I organized these chapters by a list of items and included their associated colors and intentions.

As you read through the chapters, knowing the intentions of certain items can open the door to endless possibilities that you never thought were possible. This is why when reading this book, I ask you to keep an open mind. If you have a preferred item, please feel free to use it and start your own traditions. For more guidance on how to use these items for magical work, read Part Four. I've included more information on colors as well as how outside influences can enhance your magical work.

Part Four also includes a chapter on cleansing your home. As I stated earlier, this book is not about spell casting but about keeping positive energy flowing. Keep in mind, if you have a bad day, you bring that energy home just as much as if you had a good day.

The walls of your home absorb everything you project, be it bad or good. Think of yourself as a pad of stickie notes. If you have a bad day, one of those notes travels from you and goes up on your wall, then more the next day. Before you know it, your wall is full of these negative notes, thus making you and your home stagnant. This stagnation is due to your own and other's negativity. And because you fight against yourself and those who oppose and challenge you, removing those negative notes is a hard battle.

Common items such as produce, drinks, and housewares can help you accomplish magical intent. Your supermarket is a good first place to find these items. As you build up your pantry, let *A Cart Full of Magic* be the key to the stability you always wanted for your home, your family, and you.

Part Two

FOOD, DRINK, AND MORE

✓ HEALING POWERS

✓ HAPPINESS

✓ CONCENTRATION

✓ LOVE

✓ PROTECTION

VEGETABLES

Vegetables are one of the top five food groups. They are full of nutrients and filled with vitamins A and C, potassium, fiber, and folic acid, not to mention being low in fat and calories. Their health benefits are endless, and by making them a part of your daily diet, you will most likely have a more active and vital lifestyle.

The produce aisle is full of wonderful passive and active energies. A vegetable's alchemic spiritual meanings are countless. Each one vibrates to its own frequency of love, health, happiness, or protection to bring a needed effect.

A dear friend long ago told me to make sure my plate was always full of colorful vegetables, as the more there were, the more nutrients I was sure to absorb. What she didn't know was that vegetables are perfect to start your grocer's magical journey. They are easy to manipulate and use. You can steam and bake them or add them to a healthy soup recipe.

In many cases, we are what we eat, and this goes for magic as well. We are the essence of what we portray and attract. If we portray negative energy, we attract it just as much we do positive. We are all made of the same spiritual frequency that attracts flies to a picnic.

In conventional medicine, there is always a pill for something; in Chinese herbalism there is an herb for what ails you. In magic, there is always a substantial essence to cause an effect that will fill your life with hope, dreams, and happiness.

Alfalfa

Green
Money, Financial Stability

For seven consecutive Thursdays, sprinkle fresh alfalfa on your front yard and backyard.

You can also let the alfalfa dry out in a dark, airy room. Once dry, grind it with a mortar and pestle and bottle it to use as incense when your finances start to dwindle.

Artichoke
....

Green
Protection

When placed in a black decorative bowl, artichoke protects a home from intruders.

Beetroot
....

Red
Love, Intention

Place three small beets in a pink cotton cloth and strategically place the bundle under the bed of the one you wish to stay.

Juice a fresh beet and use the tip of a feather to write your love, health, wealth, or protection needs on a clean sheet of paper. (Do not reuse the beet juice, blend a new beet each time you use one for this purpose.)

Cabbage

. . . .

Green
Love Everlasting

Take off the first seven leaves of a green healthy cabbage and hold them together with a pink ribbon. On the top leaf, write the names of the couple that wish to stay together with a marker, preferably pink. Place the cabbage leaves in a decorative box and bury it. Only dig up the box if one person wishes to end the relationship, and then burn it all.

A dear friend of mine placed cold cabbage leaves on her breast to relieve the pressure before breastfeeding with remarkable results.

Carrot
....

Orange, Purple
Male Fertility, Female Fertility

Fill a flower pot with potting mix. Within the soil, bury pink and blue baby diaper pins and carrot seeds. Every time you water the seeds, visualize conception.

Eat the seeds to enhance sperm count, or place a handful of carrot seeds in a small orange drawstring bag and carry it with you for fertility.

Cauliflower
....

White
Spirituality of the Feminine

With your hands, shred two cauliflower florets. Light a white candle and place the shredded florets around it. Do this when a young woman has her first period to avoid heavy cramping, and for her to experience a normal cycle.

Celery
....

Green
Concentration

Arrange celery like a bunch of flowers and place them close to where you are studying. The celery will help you concentrate on writing or reading.

Chili Pepper
....

Green, Red, Yellow, Orange, Brown
Protection

Place four red chili peppers on the inside of the four corners of your home. The chili peppers will protect your home from negative entities. The more desiccated and shriveled the peppers become, the better they work.

Corn
......
Yellow
Wealth

Add cornhusks to the bottom of a vase, fill the rest of the vase with corn kernels, and use the filled vase as a centerpiece in the home. Change weekly if the corn is fresh to multiply the wealth you wish to have in all things that are important to you.

Cucumber
....
Green
Worry

Gather as many cucumber seeds as you can. Place them on a brown paper bag and dry them in a dark place. Once dried, place the seeds in a blue drawstring bag and keep them with you at all time. Let the seeds take your worries. When a worry appears, pick out a seed and throw it in your backyard. When you run out of seeds, start the process again, but only if you start to worry.

Garlic
....

White, Purple
One of the Five Magical Wonders—Protection

Garlic is in every household and used as a food flavor enhancer. Garlic is in practically every kitchen or restaurant on the planet. Its culinary uses are endless, and it appears in all sorts of dishes from one side of the world to the other, but its magical uses are potent and one of a kind.

These magnificent aromatic bulbs can ward away just about anything. Hang a garland of garlic in the home, especially in the kitchen or at the front door. Place some red ribbons around the garland for even more protection.

Burnt garlic peels ward away evil spirits during exorcism. Garlic opens pathways where there are none to be found.

On the first night of the Full Moon, place a few unpeeled garlic cloves on the front steps of your home and keep them there for three days. Then, take the cloves to a river and let the flow of the water open the pathways to your heart.

Ginger
....

Yellowish Brown
Happiness, Health, Money, Success

For health, place a ginger root on a white cotton cloth. Carve the name off the person who needs help and gently wrap it up and place it under their pillow.

Grind fresh ginger and add it to your bath as a beacon to attract money, and if carried, it will invite the man or woman of your dreams into your heart.

Green Beans
....

Green
Protection

For protection, display green beans in a bowl.

Green beans can also disperse negativity from the things we think we will never have or enjoy.

Horseradish

. . . .

White, Beige
Spell Breaker

Gather four horseradish plants of the same length and width. Form a star shape with the four plants. Use a white ribbon to hold them together. On a piece of paper, write the hex you believe has been done to you and slip it beneath the ribbon. Somewhere outside of your home, use a meat cutter to chop up the plants. Hold your breath and hack into them. Once they are in little pieces, bury them and never let them see the light of day again.

Leek

. . . .

Green
Love

To bring and keep two people together for always, use two healthy long green leek leaves and make an X. On a piece of paper, write the names of the people who wish to get closer.

Then wrap the paper around the leeks with pink ribbon. Dig a small hole in the ground and gently place the leaves inside. Sprinkle the petals of a single red rose on top and then cover everything with dirt.

Lettuce

Green
Headaches

There are so many lettuce varieties that is impossible to name them here. All types of lettuce are feminine in nature.

At times over the years, I found my mother with her head full of iceberg leaves and a white cloth across her forehead to keep it in place. She swore by this unusual remedy for her headaches.

Mushrooms

Gray, White
Vision and Strength

Hold three mushrooms with both of your hands. Blow on them three times and give them the vision you wish to come true, then eat them.

Onion

White, Yellow, Red
Protection, Financial Stability

It is said not to let the peels of an onion fall on the floor or to throw them in the trash can. Instead, burn them to bring protection and financial stability.

Display an assortment of onions (from the white to the purple) in a bowl to protect you and your family from the unknown.

Parsley
....
Green
Purification

Parsley ensures the purification and stability of a peaceful and happy home. Always have a bunch of parsley in the house, and display as you would a bunch of flowers. Replace when the leaves start to wilt.

Potato
....
Brown, White, Red, Purple
Regenerating

The lore of this root is admirable. Its resilience over the years is unlike any other. It has been a staple diet within all cultures going as far back as 5000 BC. It simply multiplies by replanting. Always respect this vegetable. Be thankful for its simple nutrient, as it has kept the hungry and poor fed for countless centuries. It has been said that if you carry a tiny potato in your pocket, it will alleviate pain from arthritis and all bone-related manifestations.

Compost the peels in your garden. Give them back to the earth with the thought of generating new growth for your family, be it for financial reasons, love, or happiness.

Tomato

See Fruits.

Watercress

Green
Intuition

Place a large bunch of watercress on top of a brown paper bag and let it dry out naturally in a darkened room. Once dry, use a mortar and pestle to grind it as close as you can to a powder. As you grind the watercress, visualize being more aware of those around you and your surroundings. Place the powdered plant in a saltshaker bottle. Every day, sprinkle some on your hands and rub it in as if it were a cream. Your intuition will spike to recognize those with a good heart and those with an emotional one.

FRUITS

Fruits are my favorite magical tools, and through time people have used them as religious offerings. In today's society, we have adopted the practice of giving gift baskets filled with fruit for new neighbors, or as a token of appreciation for patronage or the start of a new business relationship. The fruit represents trust for what is yet to come or what has already come to fruition.

The color of a fruit is magical. The same fruit could be sweet or sour according to harvesting times and where they were grown. Their essence is strong, fresh, and, unlike vegetables, juicy and inviting with nothing but positivity to regenerate the soul. Like vegetables, they are full of nutrients with all those wonderful minerals that our body needs to replenish our health, vitality, and lifestyle.

For your magical needs, strategically place fruits anywhere. But don't just place them somewhere without intent. Visualize what you wish the fruit to help with or do for you on a personal level for your home as you place each piece in a bowl. Fruit is also excellent for enchanted baths and are filled with love, protection, and prosperity properties.

As you approach the fruit section in your grocery store's outer aisles, breathe in their essence—they can bring out the best in people, make everlasting love a reality, or simply brighten your space. They can bring peace to the family home like you have never encountered before.

Apple

Green, Red
Love, Healing, Luck

The lore of the apple is endless. The apple is used as an offering to the Goddess. Apples bring good luck if placed inside a basket on the dining room table. They will help bring dreams to fruition, and if mixed together with green apples, will open financial pathways. If you want love, sprinkle cinnamon on top of them.

Peel three apples and add the peels to your bath water; as you soak, think of love.

Keep the seeds of every apple you eat in a month. At the end of the month, count them, and this will be the number of days before your luck changes.

I keep an apple on my desk at home and change it every seven days. It brings peace and understanding to what I want to express on paper.

Apricot
....
Orange
Love

Eat three apricots while thinking of the type of love and partner you wish to attract. Keep the pits and place them in a pink drawstring bag. Carry them with you during the day and sleep with them under your pillow at night to attract love in more ways than one.

Avocado
....

Green
Love, Beauty

If you are selling your home, place three avocado pits around your mailbox. This will make the house attractive and beautiful to the buyer.

Bananas
....

Yellow when ripe
Family Growth

Bananas in the home increase the family in numbers and bring prosperity to the home.

Blackberry
Dark Blue
Protection

These little black-bumpy fruit (as my daughter used to call them when she was little) are very protective in nature. Display them in a nice clear bowl and visualize the protection that is needed for you or for your home. Replace with fresh berries on a weekly basis.

Cherry
Red
Love, Divination

Eat cherries when studying for a test, when you need to concentrate, or when you need creativity.

With a thin silk ribbon, tie together the stems of two cherries. This represents the love you wish to forever bloom.

To bring a family together, use a blue ribbon to tie as many cherry stems as there are people living under your roof. This will keep love tight and strong from those who wish to break it.

Coconut
....

Brown-furry
Protection

Coconut is a chameleon that disguises itself as a fruit, a nut, a seed, or a liquid carrier. This makes it diverse with many genres and in magic a very versatile tool.

Place a coconut behind your front door to keep away negative thoughts and actions from those who wish you harm.

Use the milk of a fresh coconut in your bath to protect the path you have ventured on, or to cleanse negativity when you have lost your sense of direction.

Cranberry

Red
Friendship

To bring back a lost friend, hold a bunch of cranberries in your hands and wish the person you have not seen for a while to come back into your life. Then scatter the cranberries to the four winds.

Fig

Brown
Fertility

Figs are associated with fertility and help holistically build the sperm count when eaten.

Grape
....

Green, Red, Purple, Brown, Black
Intellect, Money

When grapes, especially the green ones, are placed close to the front door, they attract money into your home.

Eat black grapes to banish negativity, red to increase strength and courage, and purple to gain enlightenment. As you eat the green ones, feel positive about your finances and your wallet will benefit from the intent.

Lemon
....

Yellow
Longevity, Clearing

Every Sunday, place fresh lemons in a bowl and between them add any leaves from your yard. If you have flowers, that's even better. This will keep the home healthy and functioning down to the plumbing, not to mention keeping the inhabitants completely happy.

To get rid of negativity from metal jewelry, dip each piece into lemon juice. Take care with any metal jewelry that is not pure metal as the acid on the lemon juice can damage certain stones and adhesives.

Lime
....
Green
Protection

When you need to get rid of negative energy from within, cut a lime in half. With one half scrub your right palm and the top of your hand. Take the other half and do the same to your left hand. Remove the halves from the home and place them in an outside garbage can with the negativity they sucked out of you.

Orange
....

Orange
Happiness, Strength

The citrus smell is enough to feel that freshness has entered your home.

You cannot go wrong with this fruit. It is filled with magical properties to clear negative energy. Oranges bring laughter and happiness to the home. Make sure your house has at least three oranges in it at all times, displayed where everyone can see them.

Place sliced oranges into your bath. As you soak, keep your intentions for happiness and strength in your mind.

Squeeze an orange on your front porch. Everyone who comes in will pick up the freshness and bring their willing disposition with only positivity in mind.

Peach
··········

Orange
Wishes, Banishment

Eat a peach in front of a person whom you wish out of your life. As you eat the peach, banish that person from your space, away from those you love and from your physical self. But wish them no harm. Just wish them to go away and never be seen again.

While eating a peach, think of the things you want to make a reality and focus on one in particular. With every bite, see it and feel it happen.

Pear
·······

Brown, Green
Love, Lust

When ripe, this fruit is very sweet and juicy and has the magical power to sweeten someone into making love. Blend three overly ripe pears, then add them to your bath with thoughts of a magical passionate night.

Pineapple

Orange (ripe)
Happiness

I have very little on this sweet unusual fruit, but I do use it to brighten my day. I juice it and add it to my bath as a pick-me-up when I need to regenerate after spiritual workings.

Strawberries

Red
Love, Luck

For a happy and loving home, don't put the strawberries in the fridge after you rinse them. Leave them on a white plate for an hour. The scent will travel through your home and spread their loving energies and luck properties.

Tomato
....

Ripe Red, Yellow, Brown
Strength, Prosperity

Tomatoes have strength qualities and yet can be fragile when over-ripe. They can still provide us with the mental strength for difficult tasks if placed where they can catch the morning sun.

Place a tomato on a counter or windowsill. As it ripens to become nothing but mush, visualize your enemy's strength weaken. If your intent is for prosperity, replace the tomato every week on a Sunday.

BREAD

There is enough bread out there on the grocer's shelf to entice us all. I for one do not buy a loaf or buns unless I gently squeeze them, making sure they are soft, crunchy, and fresh. When I bring bread home, the first thing I do is eat a piece with real butter on it.

Bread signifies satisfaction, contentment, and happiness. The smell of fresh bread is inviting and irresistible, and the temptation is something a lot of us cannot say no to.

Bring a loaf of bread home and share it either hot or cold with the family, with jam, honey, or just plain peanut butter, because as long as there is fresh bread in the house, there will be laughter and prosperity. Every morning, feed the birds with a piece of bread. They will take your dreams of prosperity to those who give it.

Never leave old bread around—it means hardness of the soul and unyielding disposition to those needing financial stability.

Bread signifies the celebration of the harvest. The wheel of the season has once again turned, celebrating the harvest festival, Lammas. We use bread as an offering for the harvest and hope for yet another.

Bread

Hospitality, Happiness, Growth

Bake your own bread at home. When you let the dough rest before putting it into the oven, slip a piece of paper with your wish within its folds. As the dough rises, so will your wish be granted. Remove the paper and bake. When you eat the bread, savor what is yet to come. (see also Grains and Legumes)

DAIRY

In some cultures, the cow is sacred. Its slaughter is prohibited, and its flesh is not eaten because of the respect this gentle animal engenders.

Dairy cows are most extraordinary; they are specifically bred for milk production. Who would have thought that one animal, together with human ingenuity over decades, could become the mother of all dairy products?

Cheese

·········

All

Dreams, Prosperity

Cheese has been a part of every culture since it was first fermented, and now the variety is absolutely enormous and never ending. Entertaining friends or guests without a cheese platter or a glass of wine is unimaginable.

Cheese is a delectable pleasure we can all take enjoyment in more than once in a while. And even if you are lactose intolerant, many varieties can accommodate your sensitivity.

Cheese has been associated with dreams. Dreaming about cheese or eating cheese could mean financial stability or the acquisition of riches.

As you eat a piece of cheese, make a wish and day dream as you savor the delicious texture.

Ice Cream

All Colors and Flavors
Comfort

There is nothing historically magical about ice cream. There is no fact or fiction that has any meaning in Santería or even Witchcraft. Like bread, ice cream is a comfort food, and we tend to crave it when we are at our most vulnerable and wish to wallow in our own misfortune and loss.

I have found that it helps to indulge lightly in the things that we know are bad for us. Of course, there is nothing wrong with wallowing over a loss, a dream gone, or a relationship lost; we wouldn't be human if we didn't.

We seem to be told constantly to always stay positive, but before we can do that, we need to accept the loss. We need to dive deep into the misery of it and find the reason for the calamity. Once we reach that understanding, we will surface with a clear perspective.

Take your time to look ahead and stay positive about the future, and while in this time of enlightenment, it's okay to dig the spoon into the ice cream bowl or bucket while drowning your sorrows while you cry. But don't indulge too long. The longer you drown your sorrows, the harder it is for you to surface, and your weight and health may suffer and become a painful reminder of why you started this self-medicating journey in the first place.

Milk
·······
White
Purification

Shoppers today have a large variety of milk to choose from, including whole milk, light/low fat, skim, homogenized, pasteurized, long life, and organic. Then there is almond, rice, lactose-free, goat, evaporated, and condensed. For those with food allergies or dietary needs, there are a few choices and brands to choose from as well.

When choosing milk for magic, try to get as close to nat-ural as you can. I always choose while milk.

Throughout myth and legend, milk is the blessed elixir; the essence of the female who nourishes and placates a baby when hungry. Milk is the spirit of what is pure, epitomizing the feminine gentle essence and her caring nature.

This white blessed liquid has been mostly used in baths and purification rituals. Milk is sacred to the practitioners of Santería, and they use it to get rid of negative energy and to purify a soul that is tormented and needs peace and resolu-tion to its distress.

A milk bath is so magical that you will want to take one again and again. Adding milk to your bathwater makes you feel so whole and peaceful. A milk bath removes all that you are not from your etheric field. Bathe during a Full Moon to complement your intent. Remember, though, that milk is sacred and you should only take a milk bath when necessary.

Add half a gallon of milk to your bathwater. You can also add essential oils such as lavender and bergamot for an even more relaxing bath. As the milk and water mix, invoke your favorite Goddess and ask her to charge your bathwater with her magical essence. This will activate your self-being to connect with milk's beauty and purity.

As you sink yourself into the water, visualize whatever ails you. Give yourself at least twenty minutes in this bath (and stay in longer if you'd like). This magical water is good not only for the purification of the soul, but also for the skin as it helps exfoliate and hydrate, preventing dryness.

Pat yourself dry to seal the energy that is now vibrating through your body and do not shower for at least 12 hours. You will feel better, more relaxed and your skin will benefit from it.

Drink a glass of milk in the morning and visualize it cleansing every single orifice of your body of all that is negative and unwise.

Splash milk on the front steps of your home to cleanse and bring all that is good and pure. Envision it taking away what is not.

Soak a baby's feet in milk for a few seconds then pat them dry. This will help cleanse the soul's past lives so as not to disturb the infant while she or he sleeps and to bless the baby with the Goddess essence.

Yogurt

Plain, White, Non-diet
Renewal, Negativity, Longevity

The first thing many of us do when we go on a diet is to buy fat-free or sugar-free yogurt. We think yogurt will make us look slim and beautiful. Well, it could very well do this with hard work and perseverance.

Because yogurt is a milk product, it's all about renewal and spirituality. As you savor a bowl of yogurt, envision your body being cleansed of all impurities. Let the gentle acid wash away all negativity within you and your etheric field.

Yogurt has also been associated with longevity, and who could resist that? So enjoy yogurt while you think about its spiritual benefits, which is definitely more than a dietary implement.

NUTS AND SEEDS

You can find nuts and seeds in the inner and outer grocery store aisles. You can buy them prepacked or by weight—either way they are crammed with magical properties.

Each nut or seed has its own health benefits, and in our society they are considered our new health pill, but all in moderation. Although I can't get enough of cashews and roasted almonds, I need to remind myself to go easy on them because too much of a good thing can be bad for you.

In magic, nuts and seeds possess a masculine energy, and they are perfect for harvesting the God force, which is associated with courage, luck, fertility, and protection. Use nuts and seeds wisely. They may seem small and insignificant, but they are potent little parcels to your magical needs.

Almond
·············
Brown
Protection

Have someone with a drug or alcohol dependency eat almonds; they are said to aid with cravings and help with withdrawal.

In your office, workspace, or business, place several almonds to bring new clients to your business.

Eat almonds while you drink alcoholic beverages to safeguard from a hangover.

When carried in your pocket, almonds stop you from overeating.

Brazil Nut
....

Brown
Love

Carry around these large nuts to bring love into your world.

Place several in a bowl in the kitchen and sprinkle them with cinnamon. This encourages friendship and love in the family home or with roommates.

Cashew
....

Off-white after processing
Prosperity

When placed in a bowl, cashews bring prosperity and riches to the home.

Cashews also guard against unwanted energies and those who bring it.

Chestnut

Reddish Brown
Love

Place three chestnuts in a pink drawstring bag. Every night before you go to bed, hold the bag and visualize the love you wish to attract.

After a relationship breakup, bury several chestnuts to take away the hurt and allow you to heal.

Chia Seeds

Black, White
Growth, Abundance

Because chia seeds congeal, they are perfect to set something in stone. On a piece of paper, write what you wish to accomplish. Place the paper in a jar, fill the jar with water, and add a large tablespoon of white chia seeds. Screw on the lid. As the seeds congeal, the resolution you wish for will become a reality.

Hazelnut
....

Brown
Luck

Place a handful of hazelnuts in a bowl and sprinkle them with dukkah as you think of the luck you wish to attract. Then place the sprinkled hazelnuts in a long, skinny glass vase, or decorate as you see fit. Display them for luck near the entrance of your home.

Macadamia
....

Brown—in the shell
Strength, Grounding

This very oily nut has a lot of masculine energy. When carried whole or eaten, macadamia nuts are great for men in need of mental strength to accomplish goals and promises, especially the promises they've made to themselves.

Pecan

Brown
Safeguard

To keep your job safe, place whole pecans in your desk drawer.

Keep pecans in the home to safeguard the peace that exists there.

Scatter these nuts in your front yard to keep your home safe from intruders.

Pistachio Nut

Green, Purple
Gossip

To stop gossip, gather three pistachio nuts still in their shell. Use an extra thin ballpoint pen to write the name of the person spreading the gossip on each nut. Close the shells with thin black electrical tape and bury the nuts in the backyard. The one spreading gossip will soon stop.

Poppy Seeds

Black
Vanishing

Buy or make a small wooden box. On the inside of the bottom of the box, write the name of the person you wish to banish from your thoughts and life. Fill the box with poppy seeds and bury it.

Pumpkin Seeds

Light Green
Conception

Pumpkin seeds can help strengthen your abdominal chakra and ready it for conception. Gather a small handful of seeds from a pumpkin. Wash them and place them on top of a brown paper bag. For a few days, let them dry naturally in a dark place. Once the seeds are dry, place them in a small orange drawstring bag. Rub this bag on your tummy every day and visualize your uterus as a magnet and your ovaries as great hosts.

Sesame Seeds

Off-White

Money

These little seeds are filled with the power of multiplication, especially for money. Place two cups of sesame seeds in a bowl and within it hide one citrine crystal and one red jasper crystal. Use the bowl as a centerpiece and change out the seeds every month on the same day.

Have faith in these little seeds. The McDonald's Corporation started with one store and one sesame seed bun and is now a worldwide monopoly icon. Let these seeds work their magic.

Sunflower Seeds

Black with a White Stripe
Wish

Hold a few seeds in your hand and make a wish, then plant the seeds in the earth. As soon as the plants sprout and grow, your wish will be in the making.

Walnut

Brown
Protection

Walnuts are strong and excellent to use on those who cannot see the truth even when it's staring right at them. As you hold a walnut, think of the person whom you wish would see reason and what you need them to see. Break the shell with a hammer. Pick up the broken shell and toss it in a garbage can. Place the walnut in a glass for a day to increase clarity. The person will now be more willing to listen to the truth.

GRAINS AND LEGUMES

Grains were among the first crops cultivated. In ancient times, they were the only consumables that didn't rot away like an animal carcass would if not eaten or salted right away.

These grains were toasted and water added to form some type of paste and that paste is what we now call cereals. Egyptians and Greeks started the refinery process until the Romans got the basics right and refined the taste of bread.

Grains are used in abundance spells and in the everlasting list for prosperity spells. They have kept our stomachs full, not so much nutritionally as vegetables or fruits do, but they have kept us satisfied without going hungry in many cultures around the world for many years.

Barley

Light Brown
Money

Get four small green drawstring bags and fill them with barley. Hold them in your hands and visualize your money needs, then place them inside the four corners of your home.

Buckwheat

Greenish Brown
Protection

Sprinkle lots and lots of buckwheat outside and around your home for protection. Place a couple of groats inside your wallet or purse to protect your money from being spent on unnecessary indulgences.

Millet (Puffed)

Light Orange to Brown
Changes, Health

For healing, fill a small white drawstring bag and carry it with you and at night place it under your pillow.

Use millet to activate change in your life. Every morning for seven days, sprinkle millet outside your home. Before you leave the house, step on the grains and envision the changes you wish to make.

Oats

Off-White
Prosperity

Once a month on a Sunday, sprinkle oats around your home, and as you do, visualize your prosperity needs. Do not vacuum until the next day. On a piece of paper, write your name and your prosperity needs. Put oats in a small box and within it place the piece of paper.

Rice (Uncooked)

White, Brown, Red, Black
Prosperity, Money, Protection

Rice has many uses, but I mostly use it for prosperity. Fill a small muslin white drawstring bag with black rice and place it behind your front door for protection. Fill a decorative bowl with rice for prosperity.

Sprinkle white rice every morning where you tread and think of the money and prosperity you need before you leave your home.

Legumes
....
All types
Protection, Prosperity

The variations of legumes (beans, lentils, and peas) are broad and colorful. The health benefits of a simple legume are precious and outweigh anything else out there in that department. The most wonderful thing about legumes is that they have no fat or cholesterol.

Plant a simple legume and give it an intent, such as for a new car, a home, employment, or financial stability. Nurture this legume into seedling stage and every time you water it, visualize your need.

Legumes are also good for fertility, so carry a small drawstring bag with a variety of them inside for this purpose.

Scatter legumes in your backyard for the fairies to use to build their homes. This secures your own home because fairies never leave theirs.

EGGS

My family has been conducting egg magic for as long as I can remember, and eggs were a staple supply in Santería while I was growing up. There was always an egg placed here or there, alone, for someone's magical intent.

Once upon a time, I thought eggs were scary and haunting. This was due to the Santeria pencil writings and lines crisscrossing the eggs that were set in strategic places around our house. I was young and not yet versed on the egg's essence and properties—and did not yet understand that the pencil writings represented the intent needed. As I grew older, however, the egg became a magical tool and something I could not do without. The creation of the egg is still debated (which came first, the chicken or the egg?). I don't know and, to be honest, it doesn't matter. This oval presentation that represents fertility and rebirth is a little magical package that is a must in all homes.

Eggs intended for magic should not be eaten. The egg has two aspects, dark and white, to absorb bad energy and leave good energy. The egg is an explosive magical tool that works effectively within all aspects of magic.

When choosing which eggs to buy for magical work, make sure you use large, free-range eggs. Use white eggs for spiritual cleansing, and brown eggs for absorbing negative energy.

All eggs used for a magical intention should be at room temperature.

Eggs
. . . .

Brown
Negativity

Place seven brown eggs in a basket. Use a pencil to write a day of the week on each of them. Visualize these eggs absorbing everything you don't want in the home. At the end of each day after the family goes to sleep, take the egg of that particular day and throw it away.

Sit down in a meditative state and hold an egg with both of your hands. Visualize all that you want to let go and what you feel is holding you back. Bury that egg so it is never seen again.

Take a brown egg into a private room and undress. Rub the egg gently all over your body and visualize the negativity you wish the egg to take from you. Pay special attention to health-affected areas or places on your body where you experience pain. When finished, throw the egg at a crossroad.

White
Renewal

To absorb goodness from the egg for health, happiness, and clarity of mind, take a white egg into a private room and undress. Rub the egg gently all over your body and visualize the goodness from the egg absorbing into your body. When finished, bury the egg pieces outside and give them back to nature.

SUGAR

Sugar brings out the magic of pleasantries and social interactions; it is the aphrodisiac for all that is sour in this world. Sugar has its place in the pantry and is also a major contributor to your magical needs.

Sugar can sweeten those who are unpleasant, don't smile, and are hard to deal with. It can also affect the ones who think the world owes them something without them ever being a contributor to anything but their own cause.

White, raw, and brown sugar are the results of the different stages of refinery. White is more refined than brown, and raw is just the first refinery step. I use all types of sugar in magic. Brown sugar is sweeter because of its high molasses content. White, on the other hand, is less bitter and more for those sweet spells to sugar coat someone who is angry or just simply a sourpuss.

Sugar
....

White, Brown
Love, Attraction, Pacification

Use sugar to attract the person you think is the one you want to spend the rest of your life with. Write his or her name on a piece of paper and place that paper in a drinking glass. Fill up the glass with water and add three tablespoons of sugar. Mix thoroughly as you envision the person you want to attract. (You can also do the same to sweeten your boss for him or her to be nicer to you.) Keep the glass somewhere where no one will touch it. Each Wednesday, redo this exercise.

Use brown sugar to help sell your house or property. Every Sunday, fill a bucket with water and add 4 pounds of raw brown sugar. Stir with the vision of the sale you wish to have. Pour the sugary content around the outside of your house or property, visualizing that there is no better house than yours on the market.

16

BAKING GOODS

There is nothing better than a freshly baked cake, cupcake, or muffin with a dollop of cream or frosting. This is a weakness and temptation that lurks within many of us—and one that we try to avoid like the plague.

There is that sense of satisfaction and fulfilment when we take that first bite of a pastry or other backed good; and if it tastes good, we close our eyes in acknowledgement, leaving you totally satisfied or guilty. (I personally like to think satisfied, as there is nothing to feel guilty about when we find pleasure in the things we eat.)

We give baked goods as a peace offering or as an offering of gratitude. The effort and the gesture in which they are given is what counts. When receiving this type of offering, keep in mind that someone has gone out of their way to actually bake something with you in mind.

When making a cake for the family or friends, make the flavor the key to your intent. As the cake rises, so do the wishes you wished for. For someone to grow financially, write the name of that person on a small piece of paper and fold it into the batter. You can also do this to wish someone wealth, health, love, and protection.

Almond Flavor

Clear to Rich Brown
Protection

Use in baking for protection.

Banana

....

Dark Yellow
Growth, Prosperity

Use in baking for growth and prosperity.

Cake, Vanilla

....

See Vanilla Extract.

Carrot

....

Orange
Male Fertility, Female Fertility

Use in baking to increase fertility in both men and women.

Chocolate

....

Brown to Dark Brown
Happiness, Love

Chocolate's magical properties have all to do with love and happiness. It has been proven that eating chocolate increases the levels of endorphins that are released into the brain to reduce stress. Eating chocolate makes us feel happier and more content with our surroundings and our resolutions.

Bake a chocolate cake for someone who needs a little tender loving care in their lives, to lift the mood in those who need it, or to bring laughter into the home.

Cinnamon

....

Brown
Attraction

Sprinkle cinnamon in your baked goods to attract all good things. (see also the Herbs and Spices chapter)

Coconut
....

White
Protection

Use in baking for protection.

Cupcake
....

White (Vanilla)
Love friendships

Who doesn't love a cupcake? The flavors are endless, and as with cakes, cupcakes always bring smiles. Bake cupcakes to lift someone's spirits. Bake them for those who live in your home and coat them with colored icing according to your intent (see Chapter 36, Applying Color in Magic).

Flour
....

See Bread.

Food Coloring

See Chapter 36, Applying Color in Magic.

Ginger

Pale Yellow
Health, Money, Success

As you add ginger to your backed goods, envision the spice adding health, money, and success to your life.

Icing

See Chapter 36, Applying Color in Magic.

Maple Syrup

Dark Yellow
Love, Money

Similar to honey, maple syrup is just as sticky and great for those money and love spells. Write the name of the one you wish to attract on a piece of paper. Place the paper in a small bowl filled with maple syrup.

You can also use maple syrup in modification spells. Write the name of the one you wish to modify to do small things around the house. Place the paper in maple syrup and dry it in the sun. Your wish will be their command.

Sprinkles

Multiple Colors
Fun, Alluring

Decorating your masterpiece is the fun side of baking. With all the different sprinkle toppings available, you can create something spectacular. Use gold sprinkles for money intentions, silver for spirituality, hundreds for attraction, green for money, and pink for love.

Vanilla Extract

Rich Brown
Love, Money

Vanilla extract is deadly sweet and used in love spells. Gather ingredients and make vanilla batter. Prepare six cupcake liners. On the bottom of each liner, envision the name of the person you wish to attract. Add your batter and bake the cupcakes and give them to the one you wish to attract.

Yeast

Off-White
Growth

This incredible fungus is in our beers and is used mostly as a raising agent for baking bread and other dough recipes.

To make your money multiply, place a few copper coins in a drinking glass. Fill the glass with water and stir in a teaspoon of yeast. Change every week using different coins.

HONEY

The rich magical properties of honey have been a part of the human experience since the inception of our time on this world. This sweet nectar has been worshipped throughout history and used as offerings to deities.

Bees pollinate without even knowing that they are doing it. They land on a flower, collect its nectar and take the pollen sac unknowingly to the next. These amazing social insects form colonies and serve a queen. They are vital to the pollination process.

Mead, one of the oldest alcoholic drinks, is made by fermenting honey with water and yeast. Selected breweries still make this drink and it is now a trendy beverage. Honey was and is still used in first aid. It was used to prevent scarring in open wounds by keeping the skin moist. It was used to aid the healing process of burns by not letting bacteria penetrate the wound. My father always put honey on our minor burns.

Honey is found in some cosmetic brands and used to rejuvenate the skin. It is also found in sunscreen and lotion.

It also tastes yummy. What would a cup of herbal tea be without a spoonful of honey to sweeten its magical content?

Honey
....

Honey Brown
Attraction, Friendship

Honey should be a staple item in your pantry. Honey draws positive energy with a vengeance; it charms those we wish to attract. Honey benefits the wallet and finances; it attracts just as it is sticky. As Winnie the Pooh says, "A day without a friend is like a pot without a single drop of honey left inside."

Add a cup of honey to warm bathwater. As you sink into the tub, let the honey dissolve in the water and on your skin. Visualize what you wish to attract into your life.

If you don't have a bathtub, undress and anoint yourself all over with honey, and I mean everywhere. As you do, visualize what you wish to attract into your life. Then take a shower until the honey has totally washed away from your skin

On a piece of paper, write the name of a person who needs sweetening. Fold the paper as many times as you can, cover it with tape, and place it in a small bowl. Pour honey all over the folded paper and place the bowl up high where it cannot to be touched.

To attract what is freely given, always keep a little cap of honey at your front door.

To attract money, carry a honeybush tea bag in your purse or wallet.

VINEGAR

All sorts of vinegars are available and ready to use in salads or to cook and preserve foods, but I only use white vinegar for magic. This blend of acetic acid and diluted ethanol fermentation was established many thousands of years ago and is unchanged to this day.

Use this gentle but powerful combination around the home for cleaning and killing germs. Soak your teacups to remove the tea or coffee stains. It eliminates odors, cleans the fridge like a dream, and even prevents static in your dryer.

Vinegar is the all-rounder, not as harsh as other cleaning chemicals, and as each day passes, there are more converts to this amazing creation. People clean their windows with vinegar and water, opting for a less harsh cleaning option. But little do they know, they are also stripping negative energy and bringing in blessing into their homes, something bleach or ammonia don't do. Sure, bleach and ammonia can strip negativity, but they can't really bless anything because they are too harsh. Vinegar eliminates negative energy and blesses in such a subtle way without malice and discomfort to those who disrupt our way of life.

Vinegar (Distilled White)

Colorless
The gentle banisher

Windows are the eyes of your home; they look out to the outside and let the outside world look in. For this purpose, clean your windows with vinegar to see things clearer. Let the sunshine and light from the outside come into your home. Let in the love it offers and the good vibrations to accomplish planned and set goals.

Clean your windowsills, doorframes, knobs, and faucets while visualizing the negativity you wish to banish.

Use vinegar in just about anything you wish, just be creative: in a spray bottle, add some vinegar to water and banish dark energies while you spray all over your home.

If a child has problems sleeping, dampen a white cloth with white vinegar and cleanse their room by wiping all mental and porous surfaces with the cloth. This will strip away negativity.

OILS

Olive Oil

Yellow to Dark Green
Harmony, Protection, Healing

The olive tree had an enormous part in Greek mythology, and we need to thank ancient Greece for the cultivation of this magical and legendary sapling. Oil press artifacts have been found dating back to 5000 to 6000 BC, and we should be grateful to Athena, Goddess of wisdom and war, for planting this tree. It is one of the oldest and most fruitful trees in history. During countless centuries, the olive tree has journeyed across the globe, and now olive oil is in our everyday shopping list and basically found in the pantry of nearly every home on the planet.

This lush oil is mostly used in the kitchen and for the preservation of foods while keeping their vitamins intact. It is best used to preserve food that will be consumed in a short period of time. It is less harmful than other methods, which use sulfur to preserve foods.

Olive oil has been a part of church rituals from its inception and is used as an anointing tool during baptisms and other collective Christian rituals.

Olive branches were used over the fireplace to protect it from lightning strikes.

I love olive oil's uncomplicated simplicity, particularly when I use it to dress my candles before magic as I get ready for the intent I wish to manifest.

Add olive oil to bathwater to bring peace, harmony, and fertility to all things within your world, not to mention it is a natural moisturizer that leaves your skin as soft as silk.

Other Oils

The following oils are either nut or seed based. Each has its particular magical property to manifest a particular need. Add them to bathwater to activate your etheric field and stabilize and tune your chakras.

When you take a magical bath with one of these particular oils, you let their energy fuse with your own to cause an effect as they hold all their magical essences. It's a wonderful way to connect with all those natural sumptuous energies.

Almond Oil
....

Yellow
Protection

Almond oil is luxurious and moisturizing. Use it in your bath when you feel the need for protection. Let its magical properties penetrate your skin and act as an armored shield from those who do you wrong.

As you use almond oil, visualize nothing but a lucky streak coming your way to activate all those things you've been waiting for to come into your life.

Avocado Oil
....

Green
Love, Beauty

What can I say about this oil that brings nothing but love and beauty to your life? Rub a small amount in your skin while gently visualizing the love you wish to attract.

Add avocado oil to your bath and let your skin benefit from its physical and magical properties.

Carrier Oils

Carrier oils are more refined; they are not used for cooking but for baths and mixing blends with essential oil. The carrier oils are softer and gentler on the skin. Some grocery stores sell quality carrier oils that are organic and 100 percent pure base oils, but read the labels. But if they aren't, don't worry too much about it; you are using these oils for a magical manifestation, not as a medical agent.

Coconut Oil

Colorless
Protection

Rub coconut oil on your skin as a protective agent against negative energy. When you do, the oil places a barrier around your body and gives you direction to where you are going or heading.

Coconut oil cleanses the aura and lifts your spirits when you are down.

Corn Oil

Yellow
Wealth

Find a small flower vase, add cornhusks to the bottom, and fill with corn oil. Place the vase as a centerpiece in the home. This will multiply the wealth you wish to have in all things that are important to you.

Grape Seed Oil

Yellow to Light Green
Money, Intellect

This subtle oil aids with your money needs.

Grape seed oil also keeps your mind sharp and in the moment, not wandering around the past, where it should not even be.

Hazelnut Oil
. . . .
Yellow
Luck, Prosperity

Hazelnut is the lucky oil. Fill a nice decorative glass, vase, or bottle with this oil, and then add a few whole hazelnuts and almonds. Place this in a high place where no one can touch it such as on top of a bookshelf.

Add hazelnut oil to your magical bath for luck and prosperity.

Macadamia Oil

························

Dark Yellow
Dreaming

Macadamia oil is excellent to use as a carrier for essential oils. Add it to your bath to make your dreams a reality. Sit back, close your eyes, and let the oil take you to the future and visualize where you want to be. It will aid you to get there.

Rice Bran Oil

························

Yellow
Prosperity, Money, Protection

This oil is for all your prosperity needs and also provides protection. Add it to your bath while visualizing the need that has taken you to have this bath in the first place.

Rose Hip Oil

Yellow to Orange
Health

When you feel a little weary, let this oil comfort your aches and pains or any other health issues you are currently addressing. Rose hip oil helps you relax while you seek medical advice. It will also help you come to terms with an illness and assist in manifesting a positive outcome.

Sesame Oil

Dark Yellow
Money

Sesame oil is thick and has a strong odor. Add a few drops only to your bathwater as you visualize your money needs.

Sunflower Oil

Yellow
Wish

Make a wish while sitting in a magical bath with sunflower oil added and holding a few seeds in your hands.

For a magical conception, visualize those wonderful yellow or orange flowers in front of you and see them activating your abdominal charka.

Walnut

Yellow
Protection

Rub walnut oil all over your body or add it to your bath for protection. It will coat the skin so no negative energy can ever penetrate from dark workings.

Wheat Germ
....

Yellow
Health, Stamina

Wheat germ is another carrier oils that is good for health and keeps your mind sharp and agile for all those business and work issues.

SALT

Salt is a simple mineral that our ancestors depended on. It was and still is one of the world's most widely and effective ways to preserve food, but it unfortunately gives food a higher sodium chloride intake. Every home has some type of salt in the pantry, and the variety found in the grocery store is endless.

In history, salt has been controversial in all countries, race, and cultures. Salt was used as a bargaining tool and even as payment for slaves. Some wars began because of salt—but why wouldn't they when salt is one of our most treasured and useful commodity. Many cultures have their own views about salt, but it certainly was and still is a major part of all of us. What all cultures have in common is that they believe salt is a vanishing agent.

In magic, we use salt as a cleanser, an astringent to our bodies that strips away all negativity that has accumulated into our conscious mind by others or that we self-inflict due to our own insecurities and mishaps. Salt is a purifier of energy, an enhancer, a device to cleanse sacred space and your magical tools.

Salt is excellent for home cleansings as it gets rid of everything negative that has come into your home through the day or week. Sprinkle salt all through the house before you go to bed, and as you sprinkle it generously, think of the negative energy you wish to vanish. In the morning, vacuum away the salt. This simple cleansing ritual will keep your home free of negativity and ready for the week ahead.

When you need grounding, sprinkle salt on a patch of dirt outside and stand on it. Dig your toes deep within the salted dirt and ask for spiritual guidance to ground your wishes, dreams, and utmost deepest desires.

For your magical bath, use any of the available salts. Taking a salt bath clears all negativity; it rips it right off your skin. Submerge all your body, including your head and hair; let the salted water penetrate every single orifice of your body while you visualize the negativity you want to get rid of. When you're done, watch it all go down the drain where it belongs, in the sewers and not on your person or in your home.

Any salt can be used for any cleansing ritual; your preference is what makes your space sacred. You will feel lighter, energized, and positively cleaner when you use this powerful natural spiritual cleanser.

All of the salts listed below are different, but they all have one thing in common: they are powerful and very handy to use for banishing and clearing space. Salt also represents the Earth element and is a grounding tool to put in place after magical workings.

Black Ground Salt

This salt is volcanic and has a pungent odor that does not transfer to food. Black salt has less sodium than table salt and is said to be better for our daily intake.

Place black salt in a bowl of water and rinse your hands to rid yourself of the day's negativity. When done, throw the bowl of water onto a road so that passing cars take it away.

Epsom Salt

There is little that this salt cannot do for you. There are at least a dozen ways to utilize Epsom salt around the home.

One of the most beneficial magical ways to use salt is in the bath, and I use Epsom salt when I do. Epsom salt not only rids you of negative energy but also has some great health benefits; it can relieve sore muscles and get rid of old flaky skin.

Himalayan Rock Salt

Himalayan pink rock salt is considered a healthier alternative for cooking, but I tend to find it saltier than all the others.

Use Himalayan salt to cleanse negativity from jewelry, especially pieces given within the family that belong to an ancestor or ones you purchased from a secondhand or antiques store. These pieces of jewelry are connected to the previous owner's essence and must be cleansed before you use them so they don't blend with your essence and cause any malicious intentions. Just be aware that salt may damage some stones or their settings.

Rock Salt

This type of salt forms in very large chunky crystals and is not used a lot in cooking as it takes too long to dissolve, so we use it on our salads and ready-to-eat meals. Use rock salt for any of the rituals listed at the beginning of this chapter.

Sea Salt

This salt is not extracted but produced through the evaporation of seawater. Use sea salt for any of the rituals listed at the beginning of this chapter.

White Refined Table Salt

White refined salt includes more minerals and chemicals such as potassium iodide, which is added to stop it from absorbing water and to stop caking.

In a bowl, add regular table salt and water, then place all the crystals you wish to cleanse. Take the bowl to your front yard and leave it out for three days and three nights. Bring the bowl back inside and program the crystals as you would normally do.

HERBS AND SPICES

The magical properties of herb and spices are endless. Their essence, just as in the flower kingdom, is everlasting. Herbs have been used for medicinal purposes since each seedling was discovered. Chinese herbalism has been around since the first century. The Romans and Egyptians also experimented with the essence and fragrance of herbs and spices.

When people plant a garden, the first thing they grow is herbs. I have to be honest: I do not possess or have the growth spirit in the garden. It seems the only thing I'm able to grow is basil, mint, and rosemary. But if you have that green thumb, utilize this gift to the fullest in your yard because that in itself is magical and a powerful gift to behold.

Herbs are the essence of Mother Nature; they give our food taste and our magic strength. The herbal kingdom is the healer of all. Some cultures nurture them not only for spiritual use but also for physical healing.

Their power is endless, magical, and beautiful. In conjunction with the Air element, we can make their essence grow and travel to enhance our thoughts and wishes. They are the best magical tools you will ever need.

A large variety of fresh herbs are available, and you may be able to find herbs in a pot ready to be planted in your garden. If you do, plant them according to the energy you wish to bring in. These fresh herbs are very aromatic and have a way of crawling inside our skin. I use them in the bath and also as a cleansing tool all over my body to rid it of negative energy or to enhance what I have already put out.

Santería uses the Water element in their magical baths with lots of fresh herbs and colognes or essential oils added. I personally love adding fresh herbs to bathwater and have had great results, not only within me but for those I recommend them for.

I use the following boiling method to extract herbs' magical properties for a more concentrated magical substance. I place the fresh herbs I'll be using in a large pot, fill it with water, and place it on the stove over a high heat. Once it boils, I put the lid on and turn off the stove. I let the water and herbs cool for a few hours and then I strain out the boiled herbs. I pour the strained water into my bathwater. Sometimes, I sprinkle fresh herbs or flowers directly to the bathwater to add other essences.

We all want a more natural approach to magic, but let's face it, it's getting harder to go back to a time when your backyard was your supermarket. But we can still find a happy medium.

A grocery store's herb and spice section can overwhelm a buyer with all the choices, but most stores only carry the popular items used in cooking and not those we frequently use in magic, which are potent and rich with magical essence. Since this book is about the items you can find in a grocery store, I assure you that I will be able to supply you with a list just as powerful to replace those favorites we love.

First, find a brand that you feel comfortable with and that is ethical according to your principles. I look at the actual herb and study the contents before I decide to get the jar or the packet, and I usually pick the one that attracts me the most.

Some herbs are so processed that they are more like a powder than anything else, but their magical content does not lessen. If your store offers an organic option, help yourself to those. I do. If they don't, don't let that stop your intent; magic works with or without pesticides.

There are a number of ways you can use these wonderful essences for your magical needs. You can sprinkle them, burn them, carry them, and even strategically place or dust them around the home.

To code your herbs, see Chapter 36, Applying Color in Magic.

Using Barbecue Coals to Burn Herbs

I have yet to see charcoal blocks that are used to burn incense and resins sold in the grocery store, but there is a way you can get around that: buy barbecue coals or briquettes. My family used these to burn incense before they discovered charcoal blocks.

To use the coals or briquettes to burn herbs, first place four coals or briquettes in a pan on the stove. Let them heat up. Use a pair of metal tongs to gently turn each one until they are close to red. Be warned they do get very hot so handle with care and let them totally cool before discarding them in the trash can.

To test that the coals or briquettes are ready, sprinkle a small amount of whatever herb you will be using over them. If they give off smoke, they are ready to use. Once you are ready, sprinkle the herb or herbs bit by bit on top of the coals. Take this smoke around the house to cleanse it, bring positive energy, and add that little bit of peace you need by blessing your space and carrying that little wish that needs manifesting.

Allspice
Healing, Money

This aromatic spice holds magical properties and attracts money. Place it on coals and carry it around the home to leave that energy happily circling.

Sprinkle allspice around the home when you have prospective buyers coming around.

Use allspice in the name of someone who has been physically or spiritually unwell.

Alum
Gossip

Santería uses the actual alum stone in magic rituals to tighten things up, from a woman's virginity to a gossiping meddler. But you can use the alum in the spice section to do the same.

Take a black drawstring bag and fill it with alum. Write the name of the person who gossips or meddles on a piece of paper and place it on something that belongs to the person in the bag. Shake it with thoughts in mind of what you want them to keep quiet about, and wish their mouths shut so they don't open them and talk about things that are none of their business.

Basil (Fresh)

Love, Protection, Money

Grab a bunch of basil and rub it between your hands until you see a green substance on them, then rub this magical essence around your heart to let love back into your life.

Arrange a bunch of basil in your home like a flower arrangement and change it every Sunday for a new one to keep the love ever flowing.

In a pot of water on the stove, bring a bunch of basil to boil. Let it sit and cool off, then empty this green water into your bath. Step into this magical water to bring money into your life.

Basil (Dry)
....

Love, Protection, Money

Sprinkle basil around the outside of your home for protection and love.

Burn dried basil on coals to bring in all those money and protection needs.

I sprinkle dry basil on my wallet to keep those coins multiplying, and I sprinkle dry basil when I'm doing attraction spells.

Bay Leaves (Laurel)
....

Purification, Strength, Protection

Burn bay leaves to be rid of negative energy or unwanted spirits.

Carry a leaf for strength when there is something you need to confront, and to give you the courage you need to face your deepest conflicts

Caraway

Protection, Health

Carry the seeds in a little black drawstring bag for protection.

Sprinkle the seeds under your child's mattress to keep away infections.

Burn caraway seeds for the overall health of your family and home.

Cardamom Pods

Love

Burn the pods to bring love into your world.

Carry them to attract the one you seek. Sprinkle them in the four corners of your home to keep love alive and strong.

Rub them between your hands when going out on the town for a love conquest.

Cayenne Pepper

Protection, Strength

Sprinkle this powerful red powder around the outside of your home for those who wish you malicious intent.

At night, dust cayenne pepper sparingly around the inside of your home. The next day, vacuum to pick up negativity from those who bring it to the home.

Chicory

Strength

Chicory helps you find the strength to battle the obstacles that can surface on a daily basis. Carry it in a small red drawstring bag for strength or give the bag to someone who needs strength.

When you take a bath, burn chicory in the room to isolate the weakness within you. As you relax, visualize the power that you alone possess to conquer all that stands in your way.

Chili
......

Bring out arguments

On a piece of paper, write the name of the one who has done you wrong and sprinkle chili powder on top of the name. I use this method to help the person confess the bad they have done and admit to the damage they have caused.

Cilantro/Coriander
....

Peace, Protection

Burn cilantro on coals to bring peace and health to your home.

Hang a bunch of fresh cilantro tied with a red ribbon inside your front door to protect your home from the neighbor's noise. Cilantro will also bring peace to the household from those who do not get along.

Cinnamon (Ground and Sticks)

·······················

Love, Success, Attraction, the Fruition of Dreams

I love to use cinnamon in most of my spells because it gives the spell power and strength to manifest. Its scent is intoxicating and attractive in a magnetic sort of way.

Without anyone knowing, place the tiniest piece of cinnamon in your mouth when on a job interview or when you are talking to the one you seek love from and try not to chew it or savor it in their presence.

Carry a cinnamon stick to attract all that you wish.

Dust your wallet with cinnamon for success in all money matters.

Place a small amount under your pillow to see your dreams become a reality.

Wrap a few sticks with a decorative ribbon and place in your room to keep love flowing.

Cloves (whole)
....
Love, Protection, Money

I love these small aromatic spices that look like rusty nails. Their scent is not as strong or as sweet as cinnamon, but they are just as powerful and change the taste of any recipe with the tiniest piece.

Place a handful of cloves around a candle for money.

Place under the pillow or in the pocket of the one you love so he or she will always be with you.

Carry a green drawstring bag filled with whole cloves to amplify the dollar situation.

Sniff the clove jar every morning to carry that essence with you throughout the day and remember the magic and the intention you are wishing for.

Cumin
....
Protection

Burn cumin seeds on coals for protection. Carry the seeds with you when you know you need protection. Sprinkle them under your car seat to keep you and your loved ones safe on the road.

Curry Powder
....
Protection

Dust inside your shoes for protection against those with poor work ethics.

To stay on the defensive when needed, place your finger inside the bottle and then bring it to your chest and draw the pentagram. This will warn the one who seeks an altercation to stay away.

Dill (Fresh)
....
Protection, Money

Although it looks like a little fluffy pine tree, dill is a wonderful herb to use to protect your finances from those who seek to wear your bank balance down, and for this reason alone you should carry a small piece in your wallet.

Dill (Dry)
....

Protection, Money

Burn dry dill on coals to protect your finances from those who seek to wear your bank balance down, and carry a small amount in your wallet.

Fennel (Fresh)
....

Healing

The smell of fennel is intoxicating. Add it to your bath to heal the physical body from injuries or sickness.

Fennel (Dry)
....

Healing

Burn dry fennel on your coals for healing.

Sprinkle some under the mattress or inside the pillow of the one who is ill or needing protection from illnesses.

Ginger (Ground)
....
Health, Money, Success

Sprinkle ground ginger in your wallet or purse for financial gains.

Place two teaspoons of ginger in a small green drawstring bag. Inconspicuously put it close to your front door to attract what is yours to have.

Lemongrass (Fresh)
....
Love, Lust

For a not-so-boring sex life, place seven lemongrass stalks that have been wrapped in red tissue paper under your mattress. Change every month to keep the momentum going.

Marjoram
....
Love

As the newly wedded couple walk hand in hand down the aisle, throw a mixture of marjoram and rose petals at them to bring stability and everlasting love to their wedded life.

Mint (Fresh)
....
Protection, Money

Rub mint in your hands whenever you are around money, or before you go to the bank to attract that energy.

Keep fresh leaves in your wallet or purse and change on a weekly basis to keep the energy and to protect your finances.

Mint (Dry)
....
Travel, Protection, Money

Burn dry mint leaves on coals for your travel plans to come to fruition. Carry the leaves in your wallet or purse for money.

Hang a small white drawstring bag filled with mint by the back door to keep money in the home.

Nutmeg (Whole and Ground)

Abundance

This is another one of my favorite magical tools. Nutmeg is for anything you want to enhance or to bring to the forefront, especially within the financial gains department.

I always have whole or ground nutmeg in my home. I carry it whole loosely inside my handbag. I also sprinkle dried nutmeg on my front door and rub my hands with it to bring all that is good into my life.

Parsley (Fresh)

Money

On Sundays, bring a bunch of fresh parsley into your home and your finances will multiply with the magical essence it possesses.

Parsley ensures the purification and stability of a peaceful, happy home.

Rub fresh parsley on your naked body for its essence to vibrate with its money frequency.

Parsley (Dry)

Money

Burn dry parsley on coals for money and take the smoke all over the house while visualizing your money needs. Sprinkle some inside your purse or wallet, in your shoes, and by your front door.

Pepper (Black, Brown, White, Peppercorn)

Repellent

It doesn't matter if you use black or white, ground or powder or the actual corns; to me all forms of pepper work as a repellent. From what I have gathered over the years and heard through the family magical grapevine, pepper was used to cause fights. You would sprinkle it around the ones you wanted to fight when they were standing together.

I use pepper as a repellent to negative magic. On a piece of paper, write the name of the person you know has hexed you, then sprinkle black pepper on top of the name. Light a match and burn it and the spell will be broken.

Rosemary (Fresh, Dry, or Oil)

Everything you can think of

Rosemary is the Jedi, the Luke Skywalker of all the herbs. I have rosemary in pots and jars all over my house. This is the herb that replaces the one you can't find when doing any spell. Use your imagination with rosemary. Every time I see a fresh bunch, I touch its leaves and then place my hands behind my neck. That intoxicating essence clears my head like no other. I also place this herb over red-hot coals and take its aroma all over the house to cleanse negative energy.

Strategically place small bunches of rosemary around the house for protection.

Carry a few leaves inside your wallet for money.

Add rosemary to a bath to enhance health and vitality.

Rub rosemary on your hands before you go out on a first date for a promising relationship and wait for your wish to manifest.

Saffron
Psychic Powers, Healing

Use this reddish yellow spice as incense when conducting magical work or meditation for a more spiritual outcome.

When doing psychometry or any healing work such as reiki, rub saffron between your hands for a clear picture between you and your client.

Sage (Fresh and Dry)
Protection, Cleansing, Healing, Purifying

Sage is one of the most trusted herbs, and largely used by those who spiritually cleanse their home on a regular basis.

Sage is the Harry Potter of the herbs and used for all sorts of spiritual and magical needs. I usually buy fresh sage and dry it, and then make my own smudge sticks. I light the sticks and take them around the house mainly to purify space.

Inhale its scent when you have difficulty making a decision. Sage clears the mind from the turmoil of knowing which decision is right or wrong; but in saying that, there are no right or wrong decisions. Every decision just makes us move forward to the next part of our spiritual journey.

I carry a few sage leaves when going to a job interview.

Put a leaf in each shoe before you get on a plane for a safe and fun journey.

In a white drawstring bag, place some dry sage leaves and give to the one who is sick to carry around for better health and happiness.

Star Anise

Luck, Healing Powers

This scented aniseed herb looks like a many-pointed star and its scent is sweet yet refreshing. Star anise is great for healing and luck. I boil three of the stars and make a tea, which I drink cold over ice to help with my digestive system.

Carry some in your wallet or purse always and strategically place them around the house during the winter cold and flu season months. It will not only keep away colds but also bring luck into your home.

Tarragon (Fresh)

Healing the Feminine

Place a fresh bunch of tarragon in a white pillowcase under your pillow to heal from a broken heart and to find the strength to deal with spiritual and feminine health issues.

Thyme (Fresh)
....
Healing

I love to add fresh thyme to my magical bath when I'm not recovering well after a cold or an illness. A thyme bath gives me that healing energy I need. If you want to use thyme in your bath, add it at least once a week for three, five, or seven weeks. I can assure you, you will start to feel better hours after the first bath.

Thyme (Dry)
....
Healing

Get a white drawstring bag and fill it with dried thyme. Give the filled bag to the one who needs physical or emotional healing. Place the bag under the pillow to give you that sense of peace, knowing that with every breath you take, you are healing emotionally and physically and becoming a stronger, more positive individual.

Turmeric

Purification, Protection

I do love turmeric but in small doses. This yellow powder seems to love my kitchen bench and appliances. I seem to make such a splatter every time I use it, thus leaving yellow marks that eventually come out. But no matter the mess, turmeric is an excellent spice for protection and to purify the family space.

Mix half a teaspoon of turmeric with a few drops of water and stir until you have a paste. If you can't get the consistency right, keep adding powder and water until you have a rich, thick, creamy paste. Use the paste to make a circle at your front and back doorsteps to protect your home. Do this on a Sunday and redo every Sunday after that to keep away those who wish you no happiness or love.

COFFEE AND TEA

Many of us enter the tea and coffee aisle on a weekly basis, and some of us cannot function without its contents. This aisle offers comfort and reflection on the coming of a new day or at the end of the day. Tea and coffee drinkers experiment with flavors and textures not to mention brands, which miraculously many seem to form a relationship with.

Tea and coffee have been a morning ritual for countless years. Regular drinkers like the aroma and the comfort they bring. We catch up with friends over coffee or tea. A cup of tea always seems to make the physical and emotional pain better. The best cup of tea I have ever had was after being under anesthetic for a medical procedure, and to this date I still have not forgotten it.

Tea and coffee drinkers have many options. There is decaf or caffeinated tea or coffee. Some like their coffee hot, others not as much. The coffee and tea culture grows on a daily basis and due to the variety, we can custom make a cup according to our taste: strong, bitter, sweet, half-strength or loaded, with milk or without.

Some grocery stores have a coffee or tea bar in their store. I have seen people shop early in the morning, sipping on a paper cup, totally immersed with the drink, like an aphrodisiac to fuel their energy sensors to commence the day.

My father cannot go without his three short espressos a day, and when he doesn't have them, he suffers from migraines. Needless to say, these drinks are addictive and the cravings are enormous for those who cannot go without their daily intake. And if you have a bad cup of coffee, it can ruin your morning, not to mention the entire day.

Coffee
....
Black
Banishing

Apart from drinking it, coffee has magical properties. Magical practitioners used it as a ritual stimulant. My family uses the coffee grounds on the soles of the feet to lower high temperatures with good results (seek medical advice when there is a temperature present).

Coffee stimulates the senses, and believe it or not, the first sip in the morning is a meditative one. Your thoughts are in a state of nothingness and you are in what I call the zone. This is a perfect time to make decisions.

On a piece of paper, write the name of the person who is causing havoc in your life and place it in a bottle. Add hot coffee grounds on top of the paper, screw the lid on, and shake its content. Bury the bottle in the backyard. Dig it up when the person is no longer a threat to your mental and emotional being. Open the jar and throw out its contents. But do this ritual again if the person persists.

Tea
·····

Various Browns, Blacks, Greens, Dark Yellows
Reflective, Strength

The tea kingdom is larger and more selective than with coffee. Like coffee, drinking tea is a reflection of the day or the day that is yet to come. Drinking tea is like taking a chill pill to calm the heightened emotions of the day. Others offer us a cup of tea when we are down. People believe that a cup of tea will make things better, and it does, it really does. This is why I use it to reflect and find the strength and wisdom to make my day, or the end of the day, a positive one no matter how shocking it was.

The scent of tea is hypnotic and spellbinding. When drinking any of the flavors listed below, reflect on your need according to the tea's magical properties. Smell the hot brew, let it enter through your nose and take it to your lungs, hold your breath and let it out again. Each time you take a breath or take a sip or mouthful, visualize your intention in a meditative state for that needed effect.

Anise, Star: Luck
Black Tea: Strength
Chai: Wealth
Chamomile: Peace
Dandelion: Wishes
Earl Grey: Money
Echinacea: Health
Eucalyptus: Health
Ginger: Money
Green tea: Health
Honeybush: Love, Attraction
Jasmine: Love
Lavender: Peace
Lemon (black tea with a slice of lemon): Longevity
Lemongrass: Love, Lust
Licorice: Protection

Linden: Sleep
Mint: Money
Nettle: Negativity, Banishing
Passion Flower: Peace of Mind
Peppermint: Dream Visions
Rooibos: Strength, Courage
Rose hip: Health
Sage: Soul Purification
Sarsaparilla: Money

WATER

Water is the elixir of life, and the most sacred treasure humankind was ever given. We consume it, we spill it when we cry, and we perspire it when we exercise and in stressful situations. We drink it to quench our thirst, bathe in it, water our gardens with it, clean our homes with it, and wash our clothes with it.

We can find water just about anywhere we look. Water is in our oceans, our rivers, lakes, and streams, even in the puddle of water outside our home. Water is what keeps the world turning, but the most important thing about water is that without it, we cease to exist. Water is filled with living organisms and absorbs mineral compounds. Every time there is a shift on our ocean floors, its composition changes. We can turn it to ice, and when we boil it, it evaporates and joins the atmosphere, then it makes its way down to start the process all over again.

There is usually a refillable bottle of water somewhere in the home, or on your desk at work, even children are allowed to bring a bottle of water into the classroom to make sure they stay hydrated. We take it on our walks and to the gym.

The Water element governs our emotions. Water rules our personality, which is at times hidden from all because we may feel embarrassment or shame in showing who we really are.

We go through what I call the waterworks stages in life. This is the emotional and reflective side of ourselves when we wonder if we should have done things differently in the past. But there is nothing the past can offer to the present unless it is to reflect on lessons learned.

In the grocery store, significant shelf space is set aside for water and the brand selection can be overwhelming. There is distilled water, which has all microbes removed though a distillation process; spring water is collected in a fresh spring as it flows naturally; artesian water is from wells; mineral water has traces of minerals; purified water is treated to removed pathogens; and sparkling water contains carbon dioxide. Then there is tonic, which is more like a soft drink, sweetened with quinine added to give it that bitter taste, and finally soda water, which is carbonated with low levels of salt.

I don't want you to buy large amounts of spring water to take a magical bath in, or to wash your floors with. That is a waste of our natural resources. I recommend sticking with basic tap water for most needs and using spring water for smaller magical needs.

Remember, don't be wasteful with water by letting your taps or hose run unnecessarily. If you take a bottle of water, finish it or put it back in the fridge for later. Remember, water is a necessity not a commodity and we need to treasure it for generations to come.

Spring Water

Spring water is the closest you can get to untampered water. Add salt to spring water and immerse your crystals to cleanse them.

Fill a large container with spring water and freeze. Smash the ice with force on your front porch to break a spell. Then sprinkle salt on top to let the negativity that was directed toward you melt away from your home just like the ice.

Write on a piece of paper the name of the person who is doing you wrong. Fill a glass with spring water and add the paper; freeze it to cool them down. You can unfreeze them, but only when you are ready to thaw them.

Use spring water to consecrate and bless your magical circle and your magical tools such as your athame or pentagram.

Sprinkle spring water in your home to bless all its inhabitants.

Tap Water

As you take a bath or shower, visualize the pleasure the water brings. Let the water caress your body and bring peace to your emotions and state of mind. Let the gentle spray scrub your body and take with it all that is bothering you. Feel its healing.

When you mop your floors, do it not only because they are dirty but because you are also cleaning the spiritual path of your home with the Water element that is strong, constantly active, and flowing. Visualize a bright light covering all the floor you will be stepping on through the week. Also visualize a constant love and light reflection in the days to come.

Use an upside-down glass of water to send back whatever negativity was sent to you. Do this by filling a glass of water and placing a white flat plate on top of it. Gently turn over the glass of water while holding the plate, making sure the glass is in the middle of the plate. Practice this a few times until you can turn the glass over without spilling, then place the upside-down glass behind your front door.

JUICE DRINKS

This grocery store aisle is totally out of hand and does my head in. So many brands with their colorful labels compete with each other, each one having their own version of a particular flavor. But unless these drinks are shelved in the refrigerated section, most are full of preservatives and high in sugar.

The three drinks listed below are ones I add to my magical bath for spiritual cleansing, happiness, and a pick-me-up. Use the juice drinks from the refrigerated section, not from the drinks aisles, or juice your own.

Coconut

....

Cleansing

Once again coconut is a strange one, but I added it to this section because there is such a variety of this furry nut: coconut water, cream, or milk. Use any of these three in your bath, but go with the coconut water or milk only because the tub is easier to clean once you're finished.

Coconut cleanses your aura and leaves you spiritually calm and anew. It helps you keep your thoughts positive no matter the outcome, without the negativity we seem to attract when things don't look as good as we want them too.

Add coconut water to your mop bucket when you clean your floors. This will ensure your home is spiritually fresh and open to good things.

Orange
....
Happiness

Add three cups of orange juice to your bath to brighten your week. It will help you look at life in a different way. It will give you a positive and happier disposition about all that you think is sad in your life, and it will enhance the possibility of a happy ending to the dilemma you face.

Pineapple
....
Pick-Me-Up

I juice this fruit and add it to my bath as a pick-me-up when I feel the need to regenerate after spiritual workings. It will also brighten your day and help you be a much happier person.

ALCOHOLIC BEVERAGES

Grocery stores around the world (except in my native Australia) keep light spirits such as beer and wine on their shelves for your use in your magical workings.

Beer

This fermented, yeasty drink has been around for a long time and is a staple in many homes and in every bar.

Beer is an integral part to Australians' way of life. It is positioned within society as a commercial commodity such as milk and bread. Beer is a part of our culture, where coming home to a cold one after a hard day's work out in the sun is practically a psychological survival ritual. Beer has its place in magic just as wine does. Santería uses beer for growth and wealth because of its yeast content.

Empty a bottle or a can of beer into your bathwater, let it expand your thoughts and watch them multiply with the intentions you wish to bring forth, from money, to love or happiness. Place several coins inside a glass of beer and let them multiply with your everyday visualization of money.

Wine

Alcohol, especially wine, has played a part in magic and many religions through the ages. Rites using wine go way back. In 1867, a bottle of wine was found in a nobleman's grave. It is believed to be the oldest bottle of wine ever found. The most fascinating thing about this bottle is that it still has liquid inside of it, and its content was sealed with wax. Scientists believe that the preserved liquid is the result of oil used for preservation. After hundreds and hundreds of years, it would have lost its ethanol content, so the taste of the liquid in this ancient bottle is still anyone's guess and very much a mystery.

Wine is used in rituals to induce a mind-altering state, and to consecrate tools, altars, and offerings. Herbs are added to wine to conjure spells for sexual pleasure or magical workings.

To me, white wine is more relaxing, but I have little use for it unless I'm drinking it. I use red wine in my magical workings; sometimes the cheaper the bottle the better it works. There is no need to buy an expensive label; a simple bottle of cabernet sauvignon will do.

Open a bottle of wine when you move into a new home and spill some of its content on the front porch as a blessing and offering to the home.

Add a pinch of lavender to your wine for a magical romantic evening.

Consecrate your magical tools with wine, or use wine as an offering to the God or Goddess.

When someone you care about is ill and you wish them to get better, take a bottle of wine to a running stream. Drink to their health and pour out the rest with thoughts of the sickness your loved one has. Watch that sickness be taken from their body and carried away by the stream.

Part Three

HOUSEHOLD, HYGIENE, BEAUTY, AND OTHER ITEMS

HEALING POWERS

✓ HAPPINESS

✓ CONCENTRATION

✓ LOVE

✓ PROTECTION

FLOWERS

Just as with vegetables and fruits, flowers have their own magical essence, but flowers are gentler and more mysterious. Their scent alone is intoxicating. Over the centuries, people have experimented with the essence of flowers to bring forth a scent, a perfume, that identifies someone.

I know my sister is around when I can smell her perfume, First by Van Cleef and Arpels. I can identify my girlfriend by her Nutrimetics perfume, which focuses on her eclectic personality. According to my daughter, I always smell the same no matter what perfume I wear. She says I smell like my store, which is filled with scented candles, incenses, resins, and essential oils. I just hope that is a compliment. Flowers

181

are a reminder of all that is good and beautiful in this world. They are magical in their own bright, subtle way. Their softness represents the fragility of our hidden personality that we don't like to share with anyone.

Flowers are also a reminder of the good in people. We express our apologetic nature with them, and our greatest appreciation. We send our sympathies with a bunch of flowers; we acknowledge someone's achievement or simply give flowers for the sake of giving them.

Flowers carry the Goddess energy and essence, and this alone must be respected. This is why when I see flowers at the grocery store, I want to take them all home and give them purpose to their life.

Flowers like to be useful until their last dying breath; and even then, their essence is still working. They can still be used on charcoal blocks to spread their essence in a room with an intent. They can be placed in small drawstring bags and sachets to cause an effect. They may look dead and lifeless, but their spirit lives within.

The flower kingdom is vast and beautiful but, unfortunately, I am only able to mention the most popular ones that I have actually seen in the grocery store.

There is no specific way to display flowers; just make sure to display them. At times, the store may sell flowers in pots. I suggest that you plant them in your garden, but if you can keep them indoors, that's even better. (For planting flower seeds, see Chapter 33, Seeds for Planting.)

African Violet

Purple
Protection

This potted flower is kept inside the home for protection. Their purple flowers are calming and can sooth even the most difficult of spirits.

Amaryllis
....
Pink, Red
Strength

These plants bring strength to a relationship, love to those who need it, and peace to the one who is hurting from a broken heart.

Anthurium
....
Pink, Red
Passion

If placed in the bedroom, anthuriums will bring passion back into your love life.

Bamboo

Green
Luck, Wishes

Bring home a potted bamboo and visualize your wishes while placing your hand on it. Bamboo will manifest as long as the bamboo stays healthy and does not die.

Bird of Paradise

Orange, Purple, Blue
Protection, Vigilance

When planted in the front yard, these flowers ward away evil. If inside the house, point their beak-like flower toward the front door to protect against those who enter your home with bad intent.

Calla Lily
....

Yellow, White
Intuition

Displaying calla lilies inside the home will make you more aware of the things you want to do and the reason why you want to do them. These flowers have a way of making you listen to your inner gut feeling and warning you against bad decisions.

Carnation
....

Various
Happiness, Healing

Carnation petals are tight and strong, and their longevity in a vase at times amazes me. I add the petals to a bath for healing not only the physical but also the spiritual. Their essence is a happy one and will brighten any room with their subtle energy.

Chrysanthemum

....

Various
Soothing

I cannot express how calming these flowers are, especially the white chrysanthemums. Their essence is one of patience, understanding, and trust.

Display chrysanthemums when there is grieving in the home.

They are excellent to dedicate to a spirit who is troubled and in need of guidance or to thank them for looking after your loved ones.

Daffodil

....

Various
Love, Fertility

Daffodils are happy and kind. They express love and understanding, kindness and forgiveness. Display them in the

bedroom for love and fertility. To aid conception, keep daffodils in the bedroom for seven days after sexual intercourse,
then change for a new bunch.

Gardenia

White
Love, Spirituality

The scent of gardenias alone is enough to fill a room with
spiritual energy. This is the energy of those we love who have
crossed over. This is the energy of our spiritual guides and
advisors. If we need their energy and guidance, bring some
gardenias home.

Note: I have only seen them at the grocery store sold in
small pots. When you get them home, plant them in the front
garden for their love essence.

Gerbera

....

Various
Happy

Gerberas are deep and vibrant, especially the orange and red ones. They always bring a smile to my face as I look at the simplicity of their form. Bring them home and dedicate them to those who are going through a hard time and are unhappy.

Hydrangea

....

Various
Spell Breaker

Do not be deceived by these colored cotton-ball-like flowers. There are as potent as they are beautiful. Display hydrangeas, especially the blue ones, in the home or garden to break the current of negative energy.

Lavender

Purple
Healing, Love, Sleep

At certain times of the year, you can get already potted lavender in the supermarket and, if you can, plant them in your garden. Lavender is calming and loving, not to mention healing. Place lavender under your pillow for sleep or for love (see also the next chapter on Essential Oils).

Lily

Various
Renewal, Strength

The lily's potent smell can accomplish what other flowers cannot. The lily has the ability to build spiritual strength. Place this flower where the family and lovers gather. On a piece of paper, use the pollen of a lily to write the name of the one you wish to break a lover's hex from and then burn the paper.

Place lilies where there is light; their fragrance will fill your home with love and renewed strength for the upcoming week or days. Make them a part of your grocery list for the week—they will never let you down.

Orchid
....
Various
Love

There are a large variety of orchids, and I cannot imagine not incorporating them into our love life. Men usually buy roses due to their popularity, sweet scent, and beauty, but orchids have a romantic energy around them that flows unconditionally. For a man, give them to a girl you want to date, and for a girl, carry them and let their romantic essence take this new romance where you want.

For those already in a relationship and who wish to spark that romantic energy again, display orchids in the home. Gently rub one of the petals and as you do, wish back the spark.

Peony
....
Various
Gentle, Protective

The peony projects nothing but gentleness; its essence is totally feminine and loving, but do not be fooled. Hidden and unaware to the onlooker, the peony is a force to be reckoned with, its protective essence is fearsome and unyielding.

Display a large arrangement of peonies when you bring home a new baby. It will protect the newborn from past-life experiences. Give the flowers intent. Their versatility will carry that intent to fruition.

Rose
....
Various
All-rounder

Roses are the mothers of all flowers. They are not only beautiful but also functional in all types of magic, from love to protection. They balance the emotions, lift the spirit, and bring blessing to those when given.

Place them in a vase and display them openly in the home to welcome those who visit.

Rub their petals gently for their essence to multiply and to bring joy before a gathering.

Bring them as a gift to your home, thanking it for looking after your family and those you love.

Offer them to the one who is sad and lonely and needs a pick-me-up.

Add the petals to a bath to bring peace to your soul.

Once in a while offer roses to spirit, as they are totally into flowers.

Use white roses for spirit, red for strength and passion, yellow for intuition, orange for happiness and laughter, purple for purity of the soul, pink for love and understating, and blush for harmony and peace.

Sunflower
....

Yellow to Orange
Strength, Wishes

This must be the happiest of all the flowers; its spirit is bright and understanding. Bring them home, change weekly for a solid month for wishes to manifest.

Take the petals and place them in a yellow drawstring bag with your written wish.

Once these flowers enter your home, you will notice the energy shift as they will bring smiles when you make them the centerpiece of any room.

Tulip
....

Various
Emotional Healing

Tulips are the listeners of the flower kingdom, the ones we tell our sorrows to and in turn they make emotional pain lessen.

Breathe your troubles into its petals and when the petals fall, throw them to the wind.

Display tulips when grounding is needed or when you expect a large gathering in your home, as they will lessen arguments with your guests.

ESSENTIAL OILS

Essential oils are a concentrated base substance derived from plants and contain the essence of a particular cutting. There are a number of ways to extract a plant's oil, including distillation and cold press. Once the process is complete, the fragrant oil ends up being stronger than the plant they were born into.

Plant essence has been used medically throughout history. Today, they are used in aromatherapy, which is a holistic practice that uses therapeutic application through scent.

Synthetic oils mimic the scent of real essential oils. These are not suitable for those who suffer from allergies or use for holistic manifestation. Essential oils are sacred in magic; use them to purify space and to bring a positive outcome, according to their properties, with all types of spells, from love to banishing. This is all due to their concentrated essence.

Before using any essential oils, do a patch test to determine if you are sensitive to its composition. Place a drop in your inner arm or back. If redness or any type of irritation develops, wash the area thoroughly and make a note that that particular oil is not safe for you to use.

I use many essential oils, especially in the bath because they are quick-acting and go straight to the intent I want to manifest. If you don't have a bathtub, you can still use essential oils just as effectively with the bucket method.

Add a few drops of oil of your choosing to a white bucket. Take the bucket with you into the bathroom and leave it outside the shower. Take a shower as normal, then bring the bucket in with you, fill it up with warm water, and turn off the faucet. Then stand there naked, visualizing what you need from the Universe. Hold the bucket over your head and gently let the water run all over you.

Many grocery stores carry a small range of essential oils in the pharmacy product aisle, outer aisles, or the hygiene section. Some stores only carry the most popular oils, such as lavender and eucalyptus, or a mixed blend for relaxing and the like.

Blended Essential Oils

There are essential oils blended by aromatherapy oil distributers for specific holistic practice. You can use them effectively according to their essences for physical ailments.

If you can't find a particular essential oil in your grocery store, here is a list of blended essential oils to substitute with energy similar: Aphrodisiac, Calmness, Concentration, Meditation, Memory Boost, Rejuvenating, Relaxation, Sleep, Spiritual Enlightenment, Stress Relief.

Allspice

············

Healing, Money

The scent of allspice is enough to awaken your senses. These little berries are gentle and yet powerful.

Burn a few drops on your oil burner for money.

Add it to your bath to heal the physical and spiritual bodies. It will help you understand and come to terms with your past and the demons you still hold deep inside.

Basil

········

Love, Protection, Money

Basil is an essence I cannot go without. I use a few drops in my magical baths and on the oil burner.

Add a few drops into a mop bucket to give the house that wonderful love, protection, and money essence and to refresh the energies within. Basil brings goodness and protects what we hold dear from those who want to take it away.

Bergamot
....
Calm, Happiness

This oil is refreshing and yet warm and comforting. Use a few drops in your bath to relax after a hard day at work.

Use bergamot in your oil burner to bring happiness within the home.

Sprinkle a few drops on the bed of the one who wakes up with an unhappy disposition.

Cassia
....
Spirituality, Fertility

Cassia is gentle but strong like cinnamon.

Add cassia in your oil burner as a meditating tool.

Rub your bed sheets lightly the night you are most fertile to help the conception of the child you've been dreaming about.

Cassia essential oil is excellent for those who work with animals; it helps them understand their pain and sorrows.

Cedar

· · · · · · · · ·

Money, Blessings, Cleansing

This woody masculine fragrance is magnetic and useful for the attraction of money if the oil is burned in your place of business. Add it to wallets for the same attraction.

Keep your crystals in cedar boxes and add a few drops of cedar before you close the lid. It will keep the cleansed crystals safe from other energies.

Bless your home with a few drops of cedar at the front door.

Chamomile

· · · · · · · · · · · · · · · ·

Peace, Healing

Chamomile is not only good as a tea to calm the emotions but is also good to calm the ambiance and heal discord. Add a few drops to the bath to relax from a heated argument.

Chamomile is great for those who suffer endless despair; it will help them calm their mind and spirit and enable them to think and look ahead with a positive attitude. It takes away the stress that caused the despair in the first place.

Chamomile also aids sleep if rubbed on the pillows or if you take a bath with a few drops added before going to bed.

Cinnamon

Love, Success, Attraction, the Fruition of Dreams

The essential oil cinnamon scent is like no other. Its attraction property is one of the strongest I have come across besides jasmine as it attracts our wishes like a magnet. But be warned, this is a powerful essence and may turn your stomach if you use it strongly.

Dab a drop on your clothes before a job interview or a date especially if you want to see them again.

Place a few drops behind your chair at work to attract good things from your boss.

Place a single drop on one of the corners of your pillow for good dreams to come true.

Clary Sage

Visions, Peace

Use this oil when meditating and doing psychic work. Clary Sage aids with futuristic visions and brings peace to the soul.

Clove

Love, Protection, Money

Clove is another money oil and can be used in wallets.

Walk around the home and leave a few drops, thinking of your money or protection needs.

Take a bath with a few drops of clove oil to attract the love you want.

Cypress

Healing, Longevity

This woody spicy oil is healing and loving. Add a few drops to your bath or oil burner for spiritual and physical health.

Use cypress on your oil burner to evoke the Goddess or help a relationship that needs healing and love to make it through trying times.

Eucalyptus
Healing, Protection

All households should have this oil in their pantry or magical pantry. Eucalyptus baths are essential and should be done at least once a month to cleanse your aura, help with physical ailments, and clear your spiritual path.

Eucalyptus is also an excellent tool to have around the home for protection. Add a few drops to your mop and bucket to clear negative energy.

Fennel
Healing

The smell of fennel is intoxicating, and I use it in a bath to heal the physical body from injuries or sickness. Use it to help heal the emotions of a broken heart.

Frankincense
....

Protection, Banishing, Cleansing

Make sure frankincense is always close at hand; it is an honest oil, pure and magical. This oil has the power to evoke spirit and bring what is due to the user.

Add to your bath to banish negative energy and spirits from your etheric field.

Use it as a cleansing tool by adding a few drops to a white cloth and using it to wipe doors, knobs, and kitchen counters.

Use it anywhere you feel someone has touched and you need their energy removed from your space.

Always use frankincense on your oil burner to bring protection to your home or business from other's negative influences.

Use a few drops on the cloth you keep your tarot cards or runes in. It cleanses them for your next psychic reading.

Geranium

......

Love, Health, Protection

Fresh is the word for this essential oil. It brings freshness where there was nothing but staleness.

Add this oil to the bath to bring love and health for those who seek it.

Use geranium in your oil burner to protect the home from spirit intruders, as they dislike the happy atmosphere it brings.

Ginger

......

Health, Money, Success

Dab a few drops in your wallet or purse for financial gains.

Place a few drops of ginger on a cotton ball and place it under your pillow for your health needs.

Add ginger to your bath for your money and success needs.

Jasmine

....

Love, Passion, Money

Jasmine is another of the attraction oils; it is powerful and just. Who would have thought that this sweet drop could have the power to do what others could not?

Use this essential oil in all your love and passion workings. Dab it on your wrist to attract the love you need; use it in your bath to enhance passion before a romantic night.

Use it on your oil burner to attract money or a new job or for a new sense of direction.

Jojoba Oil

....

Relaxing

Jojoba is one of the most popular carrier oils and is used to blend those expensive essential oils such as rose or sandalwood to dilute them for a cheaper option.

Jojoba is good for the bath to relax your spiritual and physical forms, not to mention it is also good for the skin.

Just submerge and let this kind and gentle oil take away the stressors of the day.

Lavender
Love, All-rounder

Lavender has been used very effectively in love spells. Dab your intimates drawer with lavender oil. Take a bath with it.

Sprinkle lavender in all the corners of your home to bring in that loving energy, especially where the family gathers.

Use small amounts around babies or young children to induce a peaceful sleep. Lavender is nothing but calming and soothes the soul after a hard, long, stressful day.

Lemon
Longevity, Clearing

In your oil burner, place a few drops of lemon essential oil every Sunday to keep your home healthy and functioning. It brings fresh things to the home, new ideas, or even concepts.

It also makes the habitants more than happy to be with each other.

Lemongrass
Repellent, Psychic Intuitiveness

This oil is strong and makes you aware of its magical properties. It sharpens your intuitive nature. Lemongrass repels all that is evil and those who wish us harm. Take a lemongrass bath to repel what you don't want and make use of it when conducting psychic work.

Myrrh
Protective, Clearing

Use myrrh for all your protection needs. It enhances your shield of armor to protect you from negative energy. Draw a pentagram on your front door with myrrh oil. Place three drops in each corner of your child's room to protect them from bad dreams and all entities that take advantage of our little ones.

Place a few drops in your mop bucket and cleanse you home. As you do, say, *"Be gone and leave my home."*

Nutmeg

Abundance

I personally have to be careful with this oil. Its magical property and scent is strong enough to knock me out if I'm not careful when I use it. I suggest you use it sparingly.

Nutmeg is excellent for any money, wealth, financial, or love abundance you may need. Visualize the need you seek and let this oil do what it does best: create abundance.

Add a few drops to your mop bucket and as you mop, concentrate on your abundance needs for your home or business.

Dab two drops on a handkerchief and carry its essence with you at all time. Place nutmeg under your pillow to keep the energy flowing through the night.

Orange
....
Happiness, Strength

This is a happy oil. Its fresh and motivating scent awakens your endorphins to a happy place where you can find the strength to do all the things you have wanted to do but have been unable to accomplish.

Take a bath with this tantalizing fragrance and let the orange essence blend with your own to activate your dreams so you can go out and get them.

Burn it in your oil burner to keep the happiness within your home.

Sprinkle a few drops on your back and front porches to bring happiness.

Patchouli
. . . .
Love, Passion, Fertility

Make the most of this oil, which is used in matters of love and fertility. In a small red drawstring bag, place a few cotton balls and add a few drops of patchouli for a passionate night. Use the same method for love. Substitute the red drawstring bag for an orange one to help with conception.

Peppermint
. . . .
Dream Visions

Peppermint not only is therapeutic for a few physical ailments, but also has its place in the magical world. Place one drop on your pillow to start then increase to two drops. This will enhance your ability to dream and retain those dreams in the morning.

This sweet minty oil is also excellent to burn when making plans to manifest those dreams you think are unthinkable.

Rosemary (The multi-tasker)

Everything you can think of

If you can't find a particular oil, use rosemary as your backup. You can burn this oil for health to banishing or anything else you need.

Sprinkle a few drops in your mop bucket to cleanse the home and bring in loving energies.

Use a few drops in your child's room to protect her or him from all that you can't see.

Place a few drops on your clothes before you go out on a date or if you want to attract "the one."

Use rosemary as a study tool, especially for children. Take it to work to keep you alert on daunting tasks. If you can't use your oil burner, place a few drops on a hanky or tissue and smell it a few times a day to keep you focused.

Rose

....

All-rounder

Pure rose essential oil is not cheap, but if you find it with jojoba carrier oil, it will be more affordable. It will still have all of its magical properties. This oil is sweet and passive, calming as it soothes the emotions in our hearts. It lifts the spirit and brings blessings to the home.

Add a few drops in your bath to find your spiritual health and patience when you have none. In troubled times, use this oil to find inner strength to help you through hard times, as it gives hope and purpose.

Rose is feminine and nurturing. Add a few drops to your clothes or burn it in your oil burner when you are around your children, especially teenagers; it helps them be more open around you. For many centuries, roses have been associated with love. It is used in magic to bring love, to keep love, and to heal from love. Use this oil wisely; it will never let you down once you set your mind on the intent you want to bring forth.

Sandalwood

....

Spirituality, Psychic Workings, Wishes

Sandalwood is not as costly as rose, but well worth the expense as it lasts for a long time in your magical cabinet. Use sandalwood for divination or with people who are seeking spiritual enlightenment because it calms the mind so it can focus on their particular issues.

Take as many baths as you can with this oil and make your wishes in a meditative state.

Spread sandalwood around your home, a few drops here and there, to make each member of the family more intuitive and aware of their chosen paths to become successful in life.

Spearmint
....
Love, Understanding

When you study, burn spearmint in your oil burner. It will keep you alert so you can remain focused, and it enables you to absorb all the information you are given.

Add a few drops to your mop bucket to keep loving energies within your home so no one will steal them.

Thyme
....
Healing

This oil is great for physical healing. It gets to the root of the problem while connecting to the spiritual reason why the physical is not communicating with your higher self.

Place three drops under your pillow to obtain that sense of knowing that, with every breath you take, you are healing emotionally and physically. Thyme helps you remember that you can become a stronger and more positive individual by dealing with past demons that hinder your spiritual growth.

Ylang-Ylang

Stress, Allure

This essential oil is sweet and alluring. It takes away the stressors of your life and helps you deal with uncomfortable situations with ease and calm.

Burn ylang-ylang in your oil burner to bring forth a stress-free environment.

Place a few drops in your bath to attract the one you want to share your life with, and let those magical energies embed themselves in every single orifice of your body to cause and manifest your desire intent.

HYGIENE AND DAILY RITUAL PRODUCTS

This section is not about the products as much as it is about what they are used for, and what the actual product smells like. Their smell blends with the intent you wish to manifest but is also why we use these products in the first place.

When you use the items in this aisle for magic, think of a positive visualization to the Universe. Make this visualization a morning or nightly ritual that can only cause a positive effect.

Ritual in magic is one of the most important phases of manifestation. It takes your intentions across the great divine and, when done on a daily basis, carries much strength and conviction.

The hygiene section in the supermarket is varied and filled with different brands in bottles or jars of all sizes. These products promise to make us squeaky clean and shine with their silky soft ingredients, so let's take it to another level. Use these products in a daily ritual to cleanse the spiritual body, the conscious mind, and those negative energies from people who seem to take what they should not.

When you're in this aisle, look at the items you need to replenish with a different perspective; try a new product if it matches your intent. Look at the scents or the mixtures of scents available. Be open to trying new brands.

Bodywash and Body Soap

Emotions, Happiness

Bodywash or body soap is an essential part of our daily routine, but as much as we enjoy a shower, at times it could be a double-edged sword. We cry in the shower to hide the tears from those we love. Some of my best emotional outbursts have been in the shower. By letting that water run down your body, you can feel the Water element taking away all your troubles down the drain, thus leaving you calmer and more together. Only when the sobbing stops are you ready to step out and look at the reason for this troublesome shower and have a better outlook.

Why not use bodywash or soap to clean yourself emotionally? As you lather up, visualize the upset that has brought you to tears and let it go down the drain where it belongs.

To aid this emotional wash, use products that are blended with bergamot, chamomile, and lemon, or use citrus-based products. They'll do the job of clearing your emotional well-being so the shower of emotional upsets will lessen and become a thing of the past.

Conditioner and Shampoo

Banishing, Protective

Our hair is tough and resilient. All that pulling, cutting, exposure to the sun, not to mention hair treatments are evidence that hair is a remarkable part of our physiology. Our follicles are active and on a constant growth cycle. Hair texture changes according to the products we use. Hair braiding was believed to be the first hairstyle and is still a major part of our personal appearance and style.

Hair is also an exposed extension of who we are. For centuries, hair has effectively been used in dark, manipulative workings, so we need to protect it from these negative workings. Hair absorbs and exudes energy, which is there for the taking by certain individuals. It was also believed that evil spirits entered the body through a person's hair.

One of the greatest pleasures is having your hair gently brushed, or for a lover to touch it. The 1958 movie *South Pacific* featured the song "I'm Gonna Wash That Man Right

Outa My Hair," which is about a girl who believed that by washing her hair, she could forget about a guy. This metaphor is terribly exciting and magically applicable. For example, when we go out on a date, we pay particular attention to our makeup, but if our hair is not perfect, it seems that all the time and effort we spent looking for that perfect dress and putting on makeup was a waste of time.

Incorporate magic into this fast-changing part of our body to banish and protect it from spiritual harm. It will protect you from negative workings and render your hair impenetrable to those who wish you harm.

Look for hair products with essences of rosemary, coconut, lime, violets, or almonds.

Cotton Balls

Healing, Comforting, Luck

I love to use cotton balls in magic. They are gentle and give out healing properties to those who need it. Display them in a bowl to bring luck. On a piece of paper, write the name of a person who is ill and place it in a white cloth. Then top the cloth with white cotton balls and fold it gently, thinking of the emotional or physical healing that person needs. Place the bundle in a quiet place, in a shaded area where a gentle breeze can touch it.

Keep cotton balls in a decorative jar in the living room and add a few drops of lavender oil. On a piece of paper, write the name of the one who needs a little peace, or needs to tune into their anger to resolve the problem. Bury the paper in the cotton balls.

Mouthwash, Toothbrush, Toothpaste
Protection, Money Communication

This part of our daily routine can be used as a communication tool and to our magical advantage. These products are filled with mint flavoring agents, which are good for protection and communication. We can use this to enhance the way we communicate with those we work with or in the home as a speech protector.

As a rule, we brush our teeth in the morning, after lunch, and at night. We use mouthwash after or during the day depending on how fresh we want our mouth and breath to be, especially on those romantic evenings or meetings.

Brush your teeth while focusing on the communication aid you need. Visualize your words flowing like a river or a cascade after a heavy rainfall. See your sentences uninterrupted by the insecurities that sometimes hold you back from saying what you want to say.

Every time you brush your teeth or use mouthwash, think of what you want to communicate. See it happen. Let your words and confidence shine in those meetings that include the acquisition of money, an idea you wish to bring forth, or a serious conversation with loved ones, without the bitter aftertaste when you say it like it is.

Toilet Paper

. . . .

Banishing

Toilet paper is an ingenious commodity, found in bathrooms in every household in the developed world with spares in the linen or utility closet. Before toilet paper, people had their own methods of hygiene and used all sorts of things, including corn husks, stones, and sponges. Much later newspapers and similar agents were used. Joseph Gayetty invented the packaged deal in 1857, and we haven't looked back since.

On a piece of toilet paper, write the name of the person who is causing havoc in your world, an unpleasant situation you wish to go away and never revisit, or past events you wish to forget. Place in the toilet and let it flush away.

Toilet paper is an excellent tool for banishing. The acidity in our urine is enough to rip away what you don't want to keep, hold, or be reminded of. Use this method for those who wish you harm. It will banish them to another place in time, so they'll never come close enough to harm you physically or emotionally.

BEAUTY

The beauty aisle is packed with everything to do with skin care and makeup needs. It is all about the feminine and what makes women look good and feel good about ourselves.

Although men don't usually use most of these products on a daily basis, they may find the information about hairbrushes, combs, and razors particularly interesting to explore and contemplate for protection and banishing.

Women have had a relationship with makeup as far back as we can count. It first started as a ritualistic practice that has evolved into a conglomerate of all sorts through the ages. Makeup has never stopped growing and evolving and now includes tattooing practices for eyes, eyebrows, and lips.

Makeup is believed to refine women, with all those bright colors that attract even those who don't seem interested. Applying makeup is an artful skill and a serious task that takes time and precision. Sometimes I see a waste of natural beauty on a heavily made-up woman, but if it gives her confidence, then good for her. This is what makeup is all about: the feminine aspects of the Goddess who lives within all of us.

Taking the time to apply makeup may be the only time you really look at yourself in the mirror. You go into a meditative state and your thoughts focus on the meticulous task. The relationship we have with makeup emphasizes self-care, beauty, and what we perceive others think about us.

Makeup can be used magically to a woman's advantage. Colors and the application of your thoughts could come in handy on many levels, especially for the intention of attraction. Make makeup a part of your magical practice and enjoy it as you apply it for an intent.

Blush or Bronzer

Both of these products are used to enhance the color of cheeks. This is what women quickly put on when they don't have much time or for a quick touch-up in the middle of the day. Women also use blusher when they feel ill and need some color to radiate health.

Bronzer gives a suntanned look while blush is much gentler and mimics the natural blush of the skin and its innocence and shyness.

When applying blush, think of the signals you want to project such as attraction, love, and passion. Don't just apply blusher, apply it with an intent, especially when out with friends and you spot that person looking for an invitation.

Eye Shadow

Eyes open the door to attraction. The eyes can allure and mystify. Within seconds, we make an overall opinion (whether true or not) of someone just by looking at them.

The eyes are the windows to the soul, and by applying eye color to them, you make a statement that you are open, honest, and ready for whatever life has to offer.

Eye shadow comes in different color tones to match every taste and eye color. Eye shadow emphasis the eyes and their mysterious nature. When applying eye shadow, think of what you want your eyes to say to those around you or those you have just met. Visualize allowing them to focus on your soul, the beauty that is within you, and the trueness of who you are.

Foundation

What would we do without foundation to cover all those nooks and crannies? Makeup foundation has the same meaning as the spiritual foundations of a home or the foundations of your upbringing. Nothing can grow with any type of solidity unless it is supported by a good foundation such as of love and friendship.

Foundation evens the skin tone and gives a stronger perception of health. It may make a woman more attractive, but it also acts as a barrier of protection to the skin. It spiritually manifests a barrier to those who would wish away our beauty.

When applying foundation, visualize your outer beauty being sheltered from those who have jealous tendencies toward you. This way, your skin is protected from those who use magic to disfigure or cause harm.

Hair and hair care

See Conditioner and Shampoo in the previous chapter.

Hairbrush and Comb

The hairbrush should be one of the most protected items in your home. The hairbrush carries your DNA within every strand that attaches itself to the brush. Our hair is sacred and often used in manipulative magic by those negative individuals who want to do us wrong, who sneakily steal when we are not looking to control or destroy our way of life.

Always keep your brush in a drawer or in your handbag. If you feel someone is after your essence, use a comb instead. A comb is much easier to clean after every use; this way, you don't leave any hair strands for the taking.

Lipstick

What would a woman do without lipstick! Women have been wearing lipstick through the ages. It gives women confidence and an overall attractiveness that expresses her own personality, as no two sets of lips are the same.

Lipstick is the epitome of beauty and attractiveness. Women apply lipstick as if they were going into battle, which means that when done, we are ready for whatever life has to offer.

Women apply lipstick before we go to work, meet with friends, or leave the house. We reapply it on a constant basis during the day, just to make sure we always look our best. I have a friend who puts on lipstick before she makes a phone call to any government offices. She needs that confidence to deal with bureaucracy with ease and poise.

It has been proven that women who wear red lipstick influence how quickly people approach them in a bar or a club, which is good to know if you are looking for that special person. Red also signifies courage and passion when you are ready to confront an uncomfortable situation or any sort of personal or professional attack.

When applying lipstick, take care to visualize good intentions as our lips are the door that unlocks and locks what we say. Speak with honor, and respect what comes out of your mouth as it will forever cement your personality.

Makeup, Eyeliner, Eyebrow Pencils

Makeup pencils refine the eyes and place emphasis on the eyebrows. This part of applying makeup is tricky and time-consuming, so use the time to visualize your life as structured as your eye makeup. See all the roads ahead in your life without any obstacles—as precise and straight as your application to the eyes or eyebrows, never veering but on a well-thought-out plan.

Makeup Remover

Removing makeup is an integral part of a nightly routine. This is when you are ready to remove all that has been clogging up your skin, including all the times you reapply lipstick and blush, or touch up your eyes. It is all deeply embedded in every single pore of your face and now is the time to give it a bit of breathing space.

As you wipe off this makeup with makeup remover, think about your day and all those things that you wish to forget or remove, especially those intense jealous stares you have encountered.

Mascara

Mascara enhances eyelashes, imitating a butterfly's wings, free and graceful, and can make eyelashes thicker and longer. We can choose all sorts of colors: brown, blue, black, even green and white according to the venue or the eye shadow color.

When applying mascara, think about those things you want to grow in your life, such as love, money, or happiness. Let this simple makeup application be the visualization of growth wherever growth is needed in your world.

Nail Polish, Nail Polish Remover

Just as we need to protect our hair, we also need to protect our nails. Animals have claws and they use them to protect themselves or to hunt. The human nail is no different, but we have evolved. They still protect our fingers from an impact, and act as a counterforce enhancing sensitivity to the fingers.

A single nail could be a magnet for dark forces to use against us. This is why we need to protect them. But don't forget our nails are also a fighting and defense tool, so use magic when applying nail polish.

Use the color chart to find what color is best suited for your needs (see Chapter 36, Applying Color in Magic). As you apply this color to your nails, visualize protection from outside influences and from people wanting to assault you physically and take more than your purse or wallet.

Think of nail polish as a protective barrier from negative forces, and with every stroke think of the protection that is needed in your world.

When using nail polish remover, think of all you have touched during the day, especially other's energies. See their essence wash away with the acetone and then start the process all over again.

Razors
....

The razor section in the grocery store can be a bit intimidating. The brands and variety of what they promise to do to the skin are endless. We do need to thank King C. Gillette for inventing the safety razor; his ingenuity has been converted to a multi-million-dollar industry.

We shave to get rid of unwanted hair and when we do, our skin feels smooth and silky. While you shave, do a positive visualization.

Men especially should use this time to rid themselves of what is causing their heart to ache, from your boss to your next-door neighbor, even that friend who takes advantage of your friendship for his or her own gain. Shave all that from your face so you can let new things in and smooth your way to a much more spiritual existence. Shaving can also make you more tolerant to others by creating a new path and leaving the old one behind.

HOUSEWARES

This aisle is usually simple, well-structured, and not as full as the rest of the store, but it does take up significant room.

Although there is nothing magical about a bowl or a plate by itself, these items can have meaning once we use them for a magical intent. Many household objects were at one time living, radiant energies that have been processed to create what we take for granted. We have become so accustomed to having them around that we are unaware of their origin or where they were birthed from. In fact, they've been centuries in the making. Respect our household items and see them as

241

they really are: fossils that have been blended and fashioned for a modern use.

For colored housewares, use the information in Chapter 36, Applying Color in Magic, to enhance your needs with the intent you want to bring forth.

Bottles

Look for one-liter bottles with lids to store water or magical essences. I fill these small bottles with spring water and add three clear quartz polished stones or crystals. When I feel run down, I pour water from the bottle into a glass and drink (do not drink from the bottle, you could swallow the crystals). I add amethyst to the water when I am stressed and pink quartz when I need an emotional pick-me-up.

Prepare these bottles ahead of time and store them in your fridge. Leave them out on a Full Moon for a more concentrated elixir.

Bowls

Bowls hold just about anything from solids, heat, to any liquid you can think of. The bowls found at the grocery store are usually generic looking but useful.

Use the bowls for mixing ingredients, displaying fruits and vegetables for magical intentions, holding scared items, and cleansing your crystals in salted water.

Fork

Forks have different meanings in different cultures, especially the three-tined forks that look like Neptune's mighty Trident. Neptune used his Trident as a weapon of war to cause natural disasters, especially in the oceans. It was said he did this when he was angry, and for this reason we can use a three-tined fork to cause movement within our emotions.

On a piece of paper, write down the name of the person or the situation that needs a bit of emotional stimulation, then place the name in a glass and add water. With a fork, stir slowly, and as you do, visualize the situation you wish to come to the forefront. Leave the glass outside overnight for a positive result.

Use this method to awake someone's feeling toward you if they haven't told you yet.

Stir up a little bit of chaos by stirring a fork in water at your place of employment and witness a restructure within the company.

In your front yard, place a fork in the ground with the tines up to absorb the energy from the elements into your home and garden.

In the kitchen, always have a fork out in the open or in your cutlery holder on the counter. This will absorb the good energies that roam around and let the point distribute it three or four ways according to the number of tines.

Glass (Water, Wine, Other)

Because I break glassware all the time, I refuse to purchase quality ones. But magic is not about having a Baccarat or a Waterford on display. Granted, I do like to use a nice glass to offer spirit, so if you think the same, use a nicer glass for your special intent. But the cost of a glass doesn't alter its purpose, which has no monetary value; its value lies in the spiritual journey that takes your intent to the Universe.

In magic, a glass is a spiritual carrier. Fill a drinking glass or wine goblet with water, dedicate it to your spiritual guide, and ask him or her to guide you on the journey you wish to undertake. Do the same thing for a loved one who needs clarity in their life.

Fill a glass with water and place a paper towel on top. Leave it outside overnight and in the morning, drink its content to bring healing energies to your body and soul.

Knife

A knife is one of the most functional magical tools and we all use one for a multiplicity of purposes. The knife engenders respect and caution. A butcher uses it to cut and fillet meat, a soldier carries one for combat and survival, even a Boy Scout has a small pocket knife.

A knife can be a positive or negative tool, but I like to use it for a positive intent to be rid of that which we don't want, or to bring positive energy into our world.

Use one symbolically to be rid of negative energy or bad spirits from your body. Point the knife toward you and visualize the knife absorbing negativity until you feel comfortable that it has gone. Then place the point in iced water or stab it in the ground to give back whatever was inside you to the earth, or back to the one who sent the negativity to you in the first place.

A witch uses a knife for ceremonial and consecration purposes. When using a knife, pay attention to why you are using it. Everything you cut or chop for a magical purpose is given a greater energy by the blade of the knife. The metal of the knife and the Earth element work together manifesting your dreams and your needs.

Mortar and Pestle

This simple implement, which has been around since ancient times, is a must in all households. It is used to crush and grind herbs or resins into a fine paste or powder. Pharmacists still use them, mainly for medicated creams.

I have seen ceramic and wooden ones in the supermarket. I use a wooden one because it reminds me of magic as it keeps the many scents of herbs and resins I have crushed and blended over the years. As I take my mortar and pestle out of the pantry, the smell is enough to ready me for my magical workings and I can identify its essence with the Goddess energy. Once you set your mind on what you want to crush or blend for a magical intent, crush your mixture gently while holding the pestle tightly and firmly. Visualize why you are mixing the concoction of herbs.

Plates

Plates are used as an offering tool. They hold the intent you need. Although there may be a few colors to choose from, select a white one for an offering plate. A simple white plate represents purity. Don't cloud the intent you wish to send out by using a plate with all sorts of different colors or designs.

Pots

Pots always come in handy. Preferably use stainless steel ones as they can take whatever you put in them, including dirt and sand. Use them to boil your favorite herbs and pour the water into your magical bath. Use your pots to make elixirs, potions, or blended scents of peace, protection, love, wealth, or happiness.

Scissors

A sharp pair of scissors can cut through just about anything but metal. We have them in the kitchen, sewing kits, sheds, bathrooms and first-aid kits. We use expressions such as cut the energies, cut the tides, cut your BS, and cut it out.

When we give birth, a pair of sharp scissors cuts the umbilical cord. This action not only marks the physical separation of a mother and child, but also cuts it holistically.

Cut unwanted and negative energies from a room by placing an open pair of scissors on top of a glass filled with water.

Write the name of the person who is doing you wrong on a piece of paper then cut that paper into tiny pieces. Burn the pieces to stop what they are doing. This action cuts the negative stream. Repeat at least once a week for as long as it takes.

Sheets
. . . .

There are all sorts of colorful sheets and covers for the bed. Grocers usually sell a limited range, but many carry the classic white. A white sheet on a bed is a sign of freshness and healing. I have a friend who made sure the bed had clean, ironed sheets on it when her kids were sick, and she still does the same today.

In spirituality, having a clean hospitable resting place gives us greater access to think more clearly, be happier, and enable new things to manifest in our world.

Wash sheets weekly or at least every other week, especially if you don't sleep alone. Sheets don't get awfully dirty with actual dirt, but they absorb dead skin cells, sweat, body fluids, and if you eat in bed, a breadcrumb here or there. And don't forget to wash your pillowcase and change your pillow every few months for that extra freshness.

When you slide into a clean set of sheets and feel the crispness of its freshness and clean scent, your entire body becomes ready for rest and sweet dreams will follow.

Linen and cotton sheets are made from natural fibers while polyester is not. Stick to cotton if you can. If you are lucky, you may find cotton or a blended cotton and polyester set. You can also get colored sheets for romantic encounters (see Chapter 36, Applying Color in Magic).

Spoon (Metal or Wooden)

Spoons are very handy. They hold liquid just as well as they hold anything else we eat. We use spoons to taste what we cook. A spoon is the utensil we seem to favor when camping. It is one of the most secure of all the utensils. A knife is sharp and thin to eat with or stir things, a fork lets things sip through, but a spoon, a spoon holds everything you put in it.

On a small piece of paper, write your wish. Fold it into a tiny bundle and place it on a spoon. Balance the spoon in a place where it will not be disturbed and where your little bundle will not fall. The spoon is now holding your dream and it will never let it fall or sip through until is fulfilled.

Spray Bottle

Look for spray bottles that already come with spray triggers. Fill them up with spring water and add essential oils or fresh herbs, then let them sit for the night outside on the ground under a Full Moon. Spray the household with this magical concoction to cause the effect that is needed: happiness, love, or money. Remember that simplicity is one of magic's secrets. As long as you use the right ingredients, there is no stopping what you wish to bring forth (see also Chapter 36, Applying Color in Magic).

Towels
....

Towels are very much needed after our magical baths. Use a white one to pat yourself dry after a magical bath. Wash it in hot water to take away the oil or other magical combinations before you use it again.

Vase
....

Make sure you always have a vase in the home. It has a simple beauty for holding a flower arrangement. From time to time, dedicate flowers to your spiritual guides for guiding you though this existence and its difficult patches.

CLEANING PRODUCTS

This is the getting rid of negative energy aisle. The items found in this aisle are fun yet serious as we venture to clean both real dirt and spiritual dirt. Spiritual dirt, which accumulates just as regular dirt does, is harmful as it can stop our physical and financial growth. It can stop love developing and block happiness in the home; it can bring health issues and could very well lower self-esteem and disturb sleep.

When you clean your home, think of it as giving the space a magical bath. Use more natural-based cleaning products when you can. But once in a while, you may want to bring the heavy-duty cleaners out from storage and thoroughly cleanse your home of negative energy. Many cleaning products are bleach and ammonia based. Fortunately, negativity and beings that have a negative essence or a malicious disposition hate the scent of these products, along with our most faithful cleaning product: vinegar.

These entities attach themselves to our essence for no apparent reason. Sometimes if they feel you're intuitive, they will stick around, their agenda unknown. Over the years, I have concluded that they have something they want to share with you, especially if you are around their loved ones.

Unfortunately, some people in this world practice negative magic, and when they use it against you, there is no stopping their wrath. Without communicating their odious motives as a normal person would, they seek negative magic to satisfy their own insecurities, jealousy, or whatever it is they have against you. They storm ahead, without warning, like a snake in the grass. They perform their dark workings behind your back and, sadly, wish you the worse life has to offer. This type of magic usually hits the finances and physical health

You can and should defend yourself against such workings. Your well-being depends on it. Get your home prepared
just in case someone does send those negative vibes. (For
more on cleansing your home, see Chapter 39.)

Ammonia, Liquid (Cloudy Ammonia)

You won't find pure ammonia in the supermarket because
this compound of hydrogen and nitrogen gas is extremely
hazardous. The smell is potent enough to knock you out.
Supermarkets offer a diluted substitute that is still strong
enough for magic.

Ammonia has been used for centuries as a magical
cleanser, purifier of energies, and for protection. Use it to
break hexes and bad intentions. Ammonia will never let you
down and is strong enough to work on those who want to do
you wrong. If you become aware of their intentions and their
doings, you must not let that happen. Do not, however, add

ammonia to a magical bath no matter how diluted it is. The substance is too harsh on your skin.

Place four bottle caps in each of the four corners of your home, then fill them with ammonia and change every Saturday. Do this when you know someone has it in for you and you need that extra protection, *but please keep the caps out of reach of pets and children—ammonia is dangerous to them.*

Use ammonia in the wash cycle to rinse and wash clothes of their energies.

Fill a bucket with water and add about four cups of ammonia. Wash your front and back porches to rid them of all that lurks in darkness.

Bleach

The compound in bleach is chlorine. We use bleach when we wash clothes to remove stains and whiten shirts that are yellowing. Bleach is used on floors and as a disinfectant to remove bacteria. Bleach strips away microscopic single-celled organisms that thrive in all types of environments. These organisms grow and reproduce like wildfire and are dangerous to our health. But these micro bacteria aren't just organic, they can also be spiritual and could cause more damage than a simple germ.

We all get those unexpected visitors whom we don't like. Some are critical and jealous. Others think everything you do is wrong and aren't afraid to tell you what they think. Then there are those who come to your home and use you as their dumping ground.

These visitors are all about themselves and do not once ask if you are doing okay. These individuals are called vampires of light. They grab everything positive from your every being, leaving you exhausted, and then have the gall to say, "I feel better when I talk to you." Of course they do; they have sucked you dry only to make themselves feel better. They leave you in a state of feebleness, ready to drop to the floor wondering why you let them in.

After a visit like this, use bleach as a negative energy stripper. While wearing rubber gloves, dip a white cloth in bleach and wring it out. Take it around the house and wipe every doorknob, windowsill, doorframe, bedpost, kitchen and bathroom counter, and anything your visitor has touched. You will strip away the negativity, which has no place in your home.

Use bleach when you mop your floors, then throw the water out into the street with the negativity you know it possesses—get that negativity totally away from your home.

Broom

The broom is sacred and the most visible symbol in witchcraft besides the pentacle/pentagram. The essence of the household broom is varied and practical. The broom has been the center of movies and poems over the years and even used as dancing partners.

The broom was at one time sacred in many cultures, and today the broom is used regularly in all households. We tend to neglect this miraculous magical tool by leaving it in the garage, in the laundry or cleaning closet, out of sight and out of mind. Let us have a little more respect for this familiar instrument. Bring it inside, away from the cobwebs and dust. You may not want to display one in the middle of a living room, but don't disregard this stick with bristles. Its magical uses will surprise you.

There are all sorts of brooms available, all with different bristles and poles. For magic intent, find one with a wooden stick and straw or cornhusks with red or blue cotton around the husks.

Place a broom upside-down behind your front door and sprinkle it with salt, wishing the person you want to leave your house to go. Say, "*If you return, it will only be for a short while.*" You can also use this method to keep away entities with malicious intentions.

Sweep the house from the back to the front door wishing all that is negative to go and never return. When you reach the front door, sweep all the dirt out of your home with strength and conviction.

For those who have nightmares, especially children, place a broom behind their bedroom door and as the days pass so will their nightmares ease.

When moving to a new home, leave the old broom behind. You don't want any of the old dirt or energies coming to the new home. Sprinkle salt on the floor or carpet of your new home. With a new broom, sweep away the salt before you move in to cleanse your new sacred space from negativity.

Mop

The mop is another tool we can utilize to the fullest. Look for a white one. After sweeping or vacuuming, mop the floors. Once you have swept up or vacuumed away the negative energy, you can now leave and seal the intent you need.

The mop is such a wonderful tool. In the Walt Disney movie *Fantasia*, a mop—well, a lot of them—had minds of their own as they danced along with their infamous buckets.

Fill a bucket with water, add half a cup of salt, and mop your floor. Visualize the grounding that is needed, from love to financial grounding.

Add essential oils or herbs to the mop bucket. Add lavender for peace, basil for money, rosemary or jasmine for love. Use fennel with eucalyptus when there are colds or sickness in the home; they bring healing energies and act as a disinfectant.

HARDWARE

Most grocery stores have a small section devoted to hardware, and only sell the essentials to repair small domestic items. When things start to break, it means there is something within your home or physical life that needs fixing. The longer you leave something broken or neglected, the more breakage will follow.

Have you noticed that when something breaks down in the home, something else breaks down soon after? I personally think these breakdowns come in threes, and there is always a price tag to get it fixed.

Fix what needs fixing. Don't let those blinds fall apart; they not only shield your home from the sun, but also stop negative spiritual forces looking in. Every step we take is always a forward one, but stepping on something that is ripped or broken, such as a tile or a ripped carpet, can only break or tear dreams and aspirations.

For glass, mirrors, plates, even socks or clothes: fix them or toss them. Everything in your home should be functional and running, especially the electrical items. If something can't be fixed, toss it. Broken or nonfunctioning items keep positive energy from flowing through.

The same goes for automobiles. If you are remodeling or working on a car, work on it. Having a nonworking vehicle in the home is not a good thing. A car takes you to your place of employment, which brings you a way to make a living. A car takes you to the supermarket, doctor's offices, and a friend's place. Having a nonworking vehicle spiritually hinders all those things. You will not be able to manifest anything you are looking forward to or go ahead in life.

Electrical Tape

Electrical tape is strong and very sticky; it is black, blue, or grey in a variety of widths. It is used to insulate electrical wires from materials that conduct energy, and in magic you can use it to seal energy.

The energy we want to seal is the energy that comes into our homes after a good magical cleansing. While good energy enters the home through open windows and doors, negative energy slithers through cracks and the corners of your home.

On every corner of your home, place a piece of black electrical tape on the baseboard. This will repel and keep away what your home does not want or need.

Hammer and Nails

The hammer is a very significant tool in magic. It is the one tool we all associate with building, along with the insignificant but essential nail that holds your home together (and is the culprit for the many tire punctures). These tools are also the building blocks of your magical needs.

If you are under the hammer at work, hang a hammer upside down to decrease your workload.

On a piece of paper, write the name of the person who has done you wrong and put the paper under a hammer.

Dip seven nails in bleach, then discreetly, so as not be seen, hammer them into your front door to protect your home from a negative invasion. As you hammer each nail, visualize your home in a blue bubble that no one can penetrate unless you pull out the nails and let them.

Lightbulb

Lightbulbs bring light into our world and can also bring spiritual light when we need it.

Look for a lightbulb with a very high wattage. On a piece of paper, write the name of the person who needs a little bit of switching on academically. Wrap the paper around the bulb, then cover the bulb with a yellow cloth. Leave it out in the sunlight, and let the Sun God enlighten this person so they become academically inclined.

Nuts and Bolts

Bolts and nuts come in all sorts of sizes and thickness. They hold two components together better than a nail. When you turn a bolt, it produces force to keep it in place and causes tension against its vertical dimension and will not budge unless you unscrew it.

The strength and tightness of a nut and bolt are ideal to strengthen a relationship that needs a little bit of care to help face what life can dish up. They can help to make the relationship stronger to withstand the heat of unpredictability, which can cause a relationship to fracture.

Screw a nut into a bolt and as you do, visualize your relationship as strong no matter the tribulations in your life.

Bury the nut and bolt under a grown tree or a healthy plant to forever keep you together.

Padlock

Many people declare their love and the promise of always staying together by displaying a padlock on a bridge, bench, or ocean view railing. But if the promise ends, they need to open those locks no matter who tore apart the relationship. If the padlock remains locked, it will forever bind them together, and they will never be able to move on.

Use padlocks for a promise, wish, or intent, and to rid yourself of an addiction.

Place a padlock in your home to protect the happiness and love within the walls so no outside forces disturb or envy it.

Rope

A rope is made from nylon or polyester, but nylon is the most common material used due to its strength and durability.

Ropes come in different colors, but white or a yellow are the most popular.

Use a rope to bind things that you need to hang on to, and to tighten your own or another's spending, drinking, or gambling. Tie three knots in a piece of rope. As you make each knot, say whatever it is you wish to tighten, and tightened it will be. Keep the rope with its now powerful intent in a safe place where no one can get it until your intent is completed.

Super Glue

This fast-acting adhesive clamps onto anything, even your skin, so be extra careful.

Use super glue for a magical intent when something in your life (such as a relationship) is falling apart. Find a love note that was written when the relationship was first born. Pluck the petals off of a fresh pink rose and glue the petals lightly to the note until all are safely fastened. Glue the edges of the note together and fold it shut. By doing this, you heal and strengthen the love that once was. Place in a warm place where it cannot be disturbed to heal the love you once had.

SEEDS FOR PLANTING

There is nothing more satisfying than watching something grow from practically nothing. We take joy in the thought that we have accomplished something extraordinary, which fuels our soul and brightens our spirit. There is no doubt that gardens are magical and the door to the fairy kingdom. Everything grows to fruition, and as things in our gardens grow, so do we grow spiritually, mentally, and even financially.

Planting and harvesting is the fundamental spirit in the witch's Sabbats, where ritual and lunar phases are a crucial key to planting (fertility) and harvesting (gathering). Your garden can be a powerful tool when it is up and running or, as I say, "Ready for magical businesses!"

Being in and attending a garden is good for your health as it reduces stress levels. Gardening is a type of exercise that improves mobility and strength, and it can also provide fresh produce and flowers, which bring physical and mental enjoyment.

Gardening has become instinct, a gift we should all practice. There is nothing more rewarding than seeing something grow from a seed to a shrubbery, a bulb to a herb or flower.

You don't need a large space to have a fruitful garden, you can plant one out on your balcony with jars and small terracotta pots. Your options are endless. You can even start with an old bathtub, old pipes or barrels, or recycled containers. The most important thing is that you make your garden as eye-catching or as functional as you want.

Seeds for Planting
·······························
Vitality, Spiritual Enlightenment

Grocery stores sell a variety of packet seeds, from vegetables to flowers. Use the information in the chapters on Vegetables, Fruits, Herbs and Spices, and Flowers to decide what to plant depending on your intent. When you find the seeds you want to plant, read the instructions and plant accordingly. Guide yourself with the seasons and lunar phases whenever possible. Keep in mind that as your garden grows so will you prosper.

The energy that exudes from a healthy garden is miraculous and it can fill you with vitality and spiritual enlightenment. This happens because you are totally submerged within its proximity. The constant contact with herbs, flowers, and greenery is enough to take away the gardener's negativity and replace it with love, peace, and happiness.

BIRD FOOD

Birds represent the spirit that lives within each of us. This is the spirit we have trouble letting out to shine. This spirit is the dreamer, philosopher, musician, dancer, or songwriter. This is our creative spirit that gives us aspirations, intuition, and creativity and feeds our soul. This is the Air element of our inner being that gives hope to our wishes and thought to our dreams.

Birds chirp musically, fluff their wings, and take flight to no one knows where, but where the seasons fit their lifestyle. Birds have their own magical meaning, and bring healing, peace, love, and laughter. The bluebird brings happiness and fulfilment, while the crow brings watchfulness and past life connections. Then there is the eagle, majestic and wise with great perception, while the magpie is obscure and filled with occult wisdom. The woodpecker has the ability to predict weather changes.

All birds will travel at length to get food, and if you feed them, they bring their wisdom to those who need it.

There are times in life when you need to glide through like a bird, gently with the wind; then there are times you need to fly against the wind to pursue what you need and want.

Bird Food

Energy Flow

Keep bowls of bird food and water in your yard, and when you see birds eating peacefully and bathing their wings, welcome them and let their spirit flow and fly through you.

Sprinkle bird food around the outer perimeter of your home if you want to sell it. It will attract buyers as much as it attracts birds.

OTHER PRODUCTS

The following miscellaneous items are true to their meaning. We use them on a daily basis, and you may be surprised how many of them you already have in your home. If you are missing a few, look for them at the grocery store and make them a part of your magical stock.

Be open to what these products have to offer. Just because they are simple, without any complexity to them, doesn't mean we can discard the action they engender, what they represent, or their purpose. We tend to discard them easily, as we do pens and buttons. Or we throw out socks that don't match only to find their pair a few months later where we least expect it. These items have many hidden meanings, and with positive visualization, they can be the key for you to concentrate on the intent you wish to bring forth. Let's call this intent a micro-meditation to the Universe or to the God and Goddess. Depending on what the item represents, it will be your key to your magical needs.

These miscellaneous items are significant to what positive visualization can truly accomplish when you put your mind to achieve a goal. Let these inconsequential items and what they represent be tools for protection, love, health, and happiness.

Analgesics

Analgesics are painkillers, considered mild and gentle, and are our first point of call for any sudden pain, be it from a headache, sprain, or arthritic joint pain. We all have them in our homes to manage chronic pain, and we carry some in our purses or wallets in case we get bombarded with a headache.

Remember, pain is a way to tell our body that there is something wrong, physically and spiritually. Next time you take a painkiller, think about the pain and visualize it gone—not from a temporary fix, but from a permanent solution—by analyzing the pain's origin and its spiritual essence.

Baby Pins

In addition to their practical use, baby pins are used at baby showers for decorations or to give as a gift to the expectant mother. Sadly, they aren't as useful as they once were when the pins were an integral part of the cloth diaper. But their meaning stands even to this day, significant to maternity, babies, and parenting.

Baby pins mostly come in blue, white, or pink. Buy the white ones when you've made the decision to have a baby. Pin one of them on the inside of your or your partner's clothes to tell the Universe you are ready for parenthood and its lifelong commitment.

Baby Powder

Baby powder is gentle and fragrant just as a child is. On a piece of paper, write the name of the person who needs a little bit of tenderness in their world. Place the paper in a small bowl and dust baby powder on top. Visualize the person feeling love and finding gentleness within their soul to forgive the unspeakable and move on.

Balloons

You can find balloons in the party section of your grocery store. Balloons are fun, especially for children, and allow the innocence in all of us to shine. I use balloons in my workshops. They are one of the easiest ways to help with letting go of things we carry deep within us and that haunt us on a daily basis.

Hold a black balloon in your hand and meditate on the things you want to let go. It could be something from the present, something in the past that is now holding you back, or something you are unable to identify that scares or haunts you. Blow into the black balloon, and let every exhalation be a worry off your shoulders. Blow in as many worries as needed. I have seen very large balloons and some small ones; it is up to you how much you need to let go.

When you're done, hold the balloon tightly by its neck. Take it outside, hold it up to the sky, and release your fingers from its neck. Let the balloon burst open. All those thoughts and feelings will disappear into open space so as not to haunt or worry you ever again. Repeat this exercise as many times as you want. Use the color selections found in Chapter 36, Applying Color in Magic, to choose a colored balloon to enhance your experience of letting go and banishing.

Band-Aids

Bandages protect small wounds from scarring and germs while the healing process takes place. When putting on a bandage, especially on children, visualize protection for the child from future falls and grazes.

Buttons

There isn't a sewing box out there that doesn't have buttons within it. These fasteners of all colors, designs, and sizes keep two pieces of clothing together. They're a fashion clothing accessory that some of our clothes cannot be without, especially those that button around our waist.

Use buttons to keep a relationship fastened without it being pulled apart. Gather a few dozen buttons from around your home or at the grocery store. Tie them together with fishing line. Every time you tie or string a button, visualize your relationship as stronger than ever before. Wear this colorful accessory to keep your relationship fastened as much as you can.

String buttons to win the heart of a daughter-in-law and give it to her as a gift. Even if she doesn't wear it, the sentiment is there and will bring you two together.

Candles and Scented Candles

Candles have been lighting our way for centuries. Their history is vast and somewhat complicated. Candle makers even went as far as using fat from cows and sheep to light our way. Then something wonderful happened: beeswax was discovered, and we haven't looked back since.

There is nothing better than candle magic. A candle is the essence of serenity, peace, and relaxation. Some of us light candles at the end of the day when we need some time to chill and relax the stressors of our day. We light them when we are taking a bath, and in memory of a loved one who has crossed over. We light them in the bedroom when making love or for the simple pleasure of having a candle's flame in the home.

Candles are the essence of our fighting spirit and the living flame within each one of us. At times that flame dwindles because we lose hope and our future looks bleak, but we can rekindle that living flame over and over again with undeniable force. The character of our strength surprises me because no matter what has destroyed us emotionally, we always seem to get up and live another day until our work here on this plane of existence is done, never veering from what our life's purpose is, or what we want it to be.

Scented candles are blended with other scents and commonly divided into categories such as sweet, which you can use for love; spice for money and wealth; citrus for happiness; and wood for spiritual workings. These are the most popular blended scents, and they can be used magically to attract and bring forth a desired effect.

Many supermarkets sell a small variety of taper candles. These candles are long and come in a variety of colors, but you will mostly find white, black, red, silver, or gold. But if they only have white candles, we can still work magically with that color.

When holding a candle in your hands, start the visualization process right away because as soon as you light it, your intent is already working. Taper candles are divided into the North and the South Pole, the top where the wick is will always be north and the base south.

For a more ritualistic method, put a few drops of olive oil in your hands and hold the candle with two hands. Visualize the intent you wish to manifest while rubbing one hand up to the wick and the other down to the base. Do this a few times while visualizing until the candle is covered with olive oil, then light it.

Light a candle for any intent. A candle is the only magical tool that is versatile and multifunctional for our desires. Light a candle for love, happiness, spirit. A candle's magical potential is like no other, so use it whenever possible to transmit your thoughts, wishes, and intent to where you desire it.

Envelopes

An envelope holds your holiday cards, a letter, and thoughts of love. An envelope can bring monthly bills as well as good or bad news. The contents of an envelope are sacred and should only be opened and read by the addressee, which is kind of mysterious. The content of an envelope is a secrecy that has been respected and protected over many centuries by carriers, messengers, and now postal workers.

Write a love letter to someone and mail it in care of the Universe, and physically put a stamp on it and send it. Use this method with other intensions such as for money, health, and happiness.

Protect a secret you don't wish to be known by writing it down, putting it into an envelope, and burying it so it never gets out.

Food Storage Container

Use regular food containers to store your magical herbs and supplies for easy access.

Hydrogen Peroxide

I never knew hydrogen peroxide was good for anything but for lightening my hair in the seventies. Needless to say, my hair went bright orange and was damaged for many months. It was never to be repeated again.

Now I use peroxide as a disinfectant and for spiritual cleansing. Look for the strongest percentage of peroxide. Empty the entire contents into a bucket of water and wash the floors of your home. This ensures you are cleansed and ready to accept into your home all the good things that life has to offer.

Jar

The Mason jar is now more popular than ever. You see them in restaurants as a trendy gadget to drink from, and large ones are used as salad containers in some places. Their meaning is simple. They hold things in them when a lid is placed on them.

A jar can hold just about anything, from chemicals to water. I use jars as a halt tool with my magical intent. A jar can hold your addiction; it can hold a noisy neighbor or a troublesome family member.

For that person who needs a little sweetening up, write their name on a piece of paper and place in a jar. Add brown sugar, cake sprinkles, and maple syrup. Put the lid on and shake until all the ingredients are blended together. Place the jar in a dark place and let it sit for a few days and you'll start to see results.

This method also calms anger, addiction, and anything you wish to sweeten or slow down. You can even use it on your partner if you feel the need for him or her to be sweeter to you.

Magazine and Newspaper

Newspapers inform us of happenings at home and around the world. Through social media and online newspapers, we keep current on the events around us, be they negative or positive. Magazines for women concentrate on fashion, and cosmetics; magazines for men, for the most part, are all about outdoor activities, cars, and watches.

Use these tools to create your own vision board. A vision board keeps you focused on specific life goals, such as that holiday or house, even that new car you've dreamed about. Cut out images from newspapers or magazines that represent your hopes, dreams, intents, and vision. Glue them onto a sturdy board and look at it daily. Looking at your vision board every day will keep your focus on your intent and be a reminder in case you forget what you are aiming for.

Think of this as a fun project, and every year take away the things that have come to be or add some others you wish to have or get accomplished. I make my vision board out of green cardboard paper for growth and prosperity. Some people spend a lot of time creating their vision boards and every single moment they spend on it, they take their wish to the Universe for completion.

There is no limit to what you can put on your vision board, or when or how to do it. Just do it—you'll never look back.

Matches

There is usually a packet of matches somewhere in the home to light our candles. We take matches to barbeques and camping trips, and there is always a box in our emergency supplies. These little red heads on a stick are amazing and full of banishing agents for the protection against negative forces that creep into your home.

The actual match head is made from potassium chlorate, sulfur, and other fillers, but the striker strip contains phosphorus and other agents. This is a powerful combination that magic cannot go without.

Light a match when your home environment feels stale and unwelcoming. Light one in the bedroom of a child who has been having nightmares to get rid of the past life experiences that haunt her or him in this lifetime.

Strike a match in the name of someone who needs a little bit of brain power to finish set tasks. This will set them up for any academic challenge with a new firepower of stored knowledge.

Needle, Thread, and Sewing Pins

Together, a needle and a thread can fix a piece of clothing or mend just about anything. This little magic duo along with pins are the building blocks of the textile industry. Today, industrial machines accomplish all they do, but it still starts with a designer pinning and sewing a creation together.

Use a needle and thread to patch things up in a relationship. Cut and stitch a heart together out of blue material, and with every stitch see the relationship mending. Fill the heart with cotton wool, fresh rosemary leaves, and a few drops of rose oil. Take this heart to the place where you both found common ground and fell in love. Use the same method with someone who is ill by making a little healing pillow. Use white material, and when finished, place inside cotton balls, thyme, and fresh fennel. Give it to the one who is ill to help them through this difficult time.

Pen and Paper

Words that are written seem to carry more weight than those that are spoken. A written testament confirms and attests the trueness of events, actions, or policies. Contracts are signed on a daily basis; billions of papers around the word are printed and signed, read, and written on.

The paper and pen industry is still with us no matter how computerized we get, and while a signature is still needed, there will always be a pen and paper to execute it.

For magical needs, use pen and paper to write the names of people who need help or who have done me wrong, and burn it or bury it to love, heal, or banish them.

On a piece of paper, write everything you don't want or need in your life. Take your time and don't rush it as this list may take a few days to compose. Think about the things that worry, trouble, or anger you. And instead of writing, "I hate work" or "I hate the way that guy makes me feel," write why you hate work or why you hate that particular person.

Once you've composed your letter, place it in an envelope, then take it outside and burn it out in the open. Let the black ashes take away your hurts, worries, and everyday stressors.

You can also make a list with a positive connotation by writing down the things you would like to have, such as love, happiness, or a home. Add why you want those things in the first place.

Pen and paper magic is strong and powerful. When writing, be precise so there is never any misunderstanding of the things you want to banish or the things you want in life.

Safety Pin

In the 1800s, Walter Hunt, a mechanic, invented the spring on the simple pin we all know and trust to hold things in place until a needle and thread become available.

The safety pin can be very protective and hold your energy within so no one can take it or manipulate it. Pin a safety pin inside your clothes while visualizing protection for your essence—and you'll also be prepared if you lose a pant or skirt button.

Shoelaces

There is no science to shoelaces. They hold your shoes to your feet or vice versa.

Use shoelaces to tie yourself to things you don't want to lose. Tie a knot in the name of your home so you'll never have to sell it. You can do the same thing so as not to lose your job. Tie a bow to hold onto your lover and to your health, wealth, and happiness. Place the knotted shoelace in a small box and place it where it will not be disturbed.

Socks

There is a limited variety of socks in the supermarket but I'm sure you have a pair at home.

Socks, believe it or not, are excellent to find lost things around the home. Tie a sock in a knot to find lost keys, wallets, shoes, coin, jewelry—you name it. Make sure the sock has its pair because if you don't, it won't work.

After you tie the knot, hit the sock on a hard surface three times as you state what is missing that needs to be found and it will be.

Tea Light

Tea lights are used mostly in oil burners, but you can use them just about anywhere. Put them on top of things or inside of things. These little five- or nine-hour candles are perfect for illuminating space.

I use them in my bathroom when I take a bath unless I am doing a magical ritual, then I use taper candles. Because tea lights are so small, you can place them in any room without any candleholders.

Use them when you want a little bit of spiritual light in the home. Once the wax has melted, add a few drops of your favorite essential oil so they become scented. Above all, dedicate them to spirit, who loves the gentle energy they manifest.

Underwear

Underwear is one of our most private possessions and something we do not share unless in extreme circumstances. The myth of underwear is still out there, but not as talked about as it used to be. There are superstitions about underwear that the older magical population still knows about and respects.

If a pair of your underwear goes missing, the first thing that comes to your mind is who would steal it, but worse is, what are they going to do with it if they did? They are probably going to use it to manipulate you somehow, and a dark magical practitioner could accomplish this.

Protect your underwear as much as you can, and if you hang around people you don't trust or who tap into this sort of magic, please count your undergarments.

Use underwear as an attraction tool by making small red bows and stitching them onto the back of your underwear where it is only noticeable to you. This attracts males or females when you are out for the night.

Part Four

ENHANCING MAGICAL WORK

✓ HEALING POWERS

✓ HAPPINESS

✓ CONCENTRATION

✓ LOVE

✓ PROTECTION

APPLYING COLOR IN MAGIC

Color cannot be dismissed within the world we live in. Color is a part of what and who we are. Color is what surrounds us, what makes us feel happy or sad, what lifts our spirits within nature.

Using color in magic enhances the intent you wish to manifest. Color identifies and expresses our personality in the way we dress, in the interior of our home, and in the color of our car. We talk about people who are green with envy or have a touch of the blues. We say people are in the black or in the red according to their financial circumstances. Our blood is red, the sky is blue, the sun looks yellow, trees and plants are green, dirt is brown (and in some places red), and the Moon can be seen as white or silver.

There are those who are totally transfixed with purple or pink. Then there are colors that make us cringe. We dress our children according to their gender. We adjust our wardrobe unknowingly to fit our mood and make decisions according to those colors.

There are public servants who even from a distance are identifiable by their uniforms; green for the army, blue for police officers or yellow for firefighters, and even though physicians wear a much more casual attire these days, they are still branded by the white coat.

Some people look terrible in certain colors, but it is not about what others like. Our bodies need to survive on an emotional and spiritual level. Our body absorbs the frequency like moisturizer and it embeds itself to our spiritual center, complementing our energy centers, the chakras.

The chakras are the seven energy life points that vibrate brightly within our celestial bodies. They are strategically located and vibrate to a particular color of the rainbow. Each energy center puts out a different frequency according to our mood and personality. Each point is awakened by the coil one, the Kundalini that lives spiritually within each one of us at the base of our spine, and like a snake, slowly wraps itself around our spine to awaken each life center. Then it nurtures each center with a manifestation of colors that few ever see.

Color is a tool we must use in magic whenever possible as it activates tenfold our intentions for attraction, love, protection, healing, happiness, money, and spirituality.

Color Meanings

When you buy items to use for magical intent, keep the color of the item in mind, be it a piece of fruit or a simple safety pin. Throughout Parts Two and Three, I suggested choosing one color of an item over another according to the color meaning and the item you are using for a particular intent.

This section contains more in-depth information about colors and their meaning. Use this information to choose items in the right color for your intent.

Black

Black is associated with death, funerals, and all that misery and sorrow have to offer. Black is a lonely color even though it represents the entire color of the spectrum. Black is a rebellious color for youth as it gives authority to their defiant nature.

Black is also beautiful and demands the power that it engenders. Black is a serious color and negotiating a business deal in a black suit or dress gives that sense of sincerity and strength (not to mention that we all look slimmer and trimmer in black).

Black can be a sedative and make you dismiss those around you. It can make you aggressive and suffer from depression. It can make you feel really negative about yourself and those around you to the point of paranoia and lack of confidence.

Black in magic wards away negativity. It's used to break spells and hexes. It protects against evil workings and brings truth to your magical workings. Black items are must-haves in all households because they protect and shield from negativity.

Blue

Blue brings tranquility and peace to the soul. Blue is the color of healing and understanding. Blue is the color of the sky and our infinite journey to the beyond. It can make you speak your mind when you've been lacking courage to speak up against injustice to others or to yourself.

Too much blue can make you overreact and speak negativity toward others and not enough blue can make you timid, shy to speak your thoughts, and resistant to change.

I love to use blue in magic; it's the keeper of peace, it calms and banishes anger. It heals as it manifests tranquility in the home. It's the color I use in protection spells as it pacifies other's initial intent, so you don't get the brunt of it. Use blue while meditating and reflecting on what has made anger surface.

Green

Green is the color that is all around us, the color of growth and prosperity. It brings luck in business endeavors and attracts money. Green balances the soul and heals your emotions by bringing understanding and creating spiritual growth.

Forget about dressing your child in pink or blue; dress them in bright green for their physical and emotional growth. This is the color for growing children so they can learn to take that first step and heal from their past life hurts and experiences.

Too much green, on the other hand, can make you angry and even jealous; not enough can make you needy for acceptance by loved ones and prevents you from making decisions that will make you happy.

Green is used in magic for financial growth and spiritual healing. Everything around us is green and in a constant growth cycle. By using green in our magical working, we can tap into the ever-growing cycle to enhance our needs.

Orange

Orange is a celestial color. Orange is the color of the armor of angels. Orange is the color of growth and conception. It promotes encouragement by activating all major organs. When meditating, it opens communications on the Astral plane.

Orange is warm and loving; it stimulates happiness and love. It gives back what was taken and its glow brightens the day.

Too much orange makes you a not-so-nice person as it makes you seek power from wherever you need it without consequences. Too little orange makes you hide within and not shine, scared of what others may think. Orange in magic opens up communication with the spirit world. It brings happiness to the home and unexpected good things and gifts you never thought were possible by promoting encouragement when needed.

Pink

No other color could be as soft and gentle as pink. It is the feminine essence in all of us, the essence of love, understanding, and everlasting friendships. Pink brings love within each of us so we can express it to attract the one we seek.

Pink brings harmony, peace, and laughter; pacifies anger; and causes affection within all in the home.

Too much pink creates physical and spiritual weakness, and not enough pink stops your dreams and makes them stagnant without manifesting because you are not happy with what you already have.

Pink is used in magic for love and self-love, to calm and pacify someone's anger or resentment, to look into the past without anger and without the poor-me syndrome, and to find love within to start to heal.

Purple, Lavender, Indigo, and Violet

I like to put these together into one color; they all seem to have the same color connotation. They all work with karma and your spiritual guides. They are all perceptive, intuitive, creative, and peaceful.

These colors slow down progressive illnesses and calm the mind to enable you to make contact with the spirit world. They create imagination and aid with the visualization of your dreams. They can help keep mental stability to the unfocused brain.

These are excellent for meditation and group psychic workings and spiritual development. They relieve stress in the home and work amazingly well with young children to aid sleep. If you need to use a color, these are the ones that will never let you down as they all work with spirit.

Red
......

Red enhances the power within each one of us. It gives you strength to fight against the odds that present themselves in our daily path. Red gives courage to our dreams. It helps us endure physical pain and strips depression when there is no clinical manifestation of its presence.

Red is the color of passion and lust that ignites the fire of our sexual urges and desires to enhance our sexuality. Too much red can cause anger and could possibly ignite resentful tendencies, but not enough red can make us manipulative, needy, and possessive. It can also give us emotional well-being and strength.

Red can be used in magic to give strength to a spell, to someone who needs that extra courage. Red amplifies the need to succeed and confront others if they have done you wrong or to stand up for yourself in every part of your life.

White
·········

White is the color of spirituality and white magic. It is the color of innocence with always a positive connotation. White is the color of peace and understanding; the color of purity and the Goddess and the simplicity within the world we live in.

Too much white can confuse the outcome of our thinking because there is never only white, but black as well, and we must work with both sides of everything in life to understand the meaning of it all while honoring who we are.

White in magic is for spiritual workings with guides or a deity. White shows respect for your magical workings and is used to contact spirit. It combats negative energy and protects against dark workings to bring justice to injustice. It's a great color for healing the physical and the spiritual.

Yellow

....

Yellow is the color of intuition, the color that makes us psychic. It can make us sensitive to other's feelings and emotions. It opens the mind to new possibilities by creating thoughts through dreams.

Yellow brings happiness to the home. Yellow is excellent for those who study and for the growing mind of children as it absorbs knowledge like no other color. It brings understanding while working with karma.

Too much yellow can make us critical and unwilling to listen to anyone else, but not enough yellow can make us timid, afraid to learn and excel in life.

Yellow in magic can help us create what we want and need. It takes our message of hope and aid to the Universe through the Air element. Yellow creates knowledge and understanding. It sparks desire and the know-how to accomplish our goal with a sharp mind, perception, and persistence.

Color in Water
....

There is a positive way to work with water, and color is one of the most effective ways to enhance your needs. Adding color to your water spells is as magical as it can get, and that includes in your baths as well.

In the grocery store's baking goods aisle, you'll find food coloring. It comes in small bottles on their own or in a pack ready for you to start your baking and icing experiences. Sometimes you can find colors already mixed so you don't have to blend them to make a specific color.

There are the primary colors of red, yellow, and blue. These are the foundations of all other colors, and secondary colors are the combination of those. Mixing color for your magical needs is fun and rewarding. It is an excellent enhancer to all your magical needs.

Blend primary colors to create secondary colors and blend primary and secondary colors to create tertiary colors. This is all well and good, but for our magical intentions we are looking for straightforward, true colors that are easy to blend.

Black: Protection

In a spray bottle, add spring water and rosemary leaves, then a few drops of food coloring to create black. Let it stand for a few hours, and then spray it all around the outside of your home for protection.

Blue: Healing, Peace, Protection

In a glass of water, add two drops of blue food coloring. Leave it out for the night, then in the morning drink it. As you drink, visualize health and peace within and protection from illnesses that may come your way.

Add small traces of blue food coloring and magical herbs to your bath to add that extra calmness.

On a piece of paper, write the name of the person giving you a hard time. Put the paper into a drinking glass, add water and a drop of blue food coloring. Stir it around and as you do, visualize the person calming down and leaving you alone. Then stick the paper in the freezer and keep them in there until they settle down. This could be done for the boss at work, a meddling mother-in-law, or a next-door neighbor. The good thing about this exercise is that it does not harm anyone.

Green: Growth
Add two or three drops of green to your bath for all your financial needs.

Add green food coloring and fresh basil to a spray bottle. Spray it around the house when finances need a boost or are dwindling.

Add green food coloring to a water bottle and store in the fridge. Drink from it and when you do tell yourself, "I'm rich within and I will attract money."

Orange (Blend Yellow and Red): Communication, Encouragement
To open communication with your deity, fill a bowl with spring water and add a few drops of orange coloring. Place

the bowl in front of you and start your meditation. Visualize this vibrant color opening the door to the spirit world with the message you wish to deliver.

Fill a bowl with spring water and add orange coloring. Place the bowl under the bed of the one who needs encouragement without them knowing and see the difference it makes.

Pink (Use a small amount of red): Love

Find a small spray bottle that you can carry in your purse. Inside this bottle, add one tablespoon (15 ml) of vodka, all the seeds from a red apple, five basil leaves, one cinnamon stick, and a drop of spearmint essential oil. Fill with water and add two drops of pink food coloring and five drops of lavender essential oil. Spray yourself with this love mixture at least three times a day to find and attract the love you've been waiting for. Re-mix the ingredients every Friday.

Purple (Blend Red and Blue): Divine, Intuitiveness

Purple is a great color for meditation, spiritual workings, psychic readings, and higher existence. For all these types of workings, use this color in tablecloths, water bottles, candles, and candleholders.

Add a few purple drops to your bath before any spiritual workings to get the energy you wish to send out flowing through the cosmos.

Red: Courage, Passion, Strength, Confrontation

Red is associated with anything to do with courage, passion, and confrontation. It gives strength and conviction to any intention.

Add red food coloring to your bath before a passionate evening.

Fill a small decorative bottle with fresh thyme, then add spring water and a few drops of red food coloring. Keep the bottle on your desk to give you courage to undertake new things, a passion for your work, strength to overcome obstacles, and professionalism if any confrontation should arise.

Yellow: Intuition, Study

Yellow is a great color when you need to buckle down with your studies. Fill a tall glass with spring water and ice; add two drops of yellow food coloring (or more depending on the size of the glass). Keep the glass in front of you and sip it while you study. It will help you concentrate and absorb every word you read or be creative with every word your write.

Add yellow food coloring to your bath when you have a decision to make to be sure you are in tune with all the pros and the cons.

Color Coding Your Herbs

Now that you are more aware of the main colors of the spectrum, let's code your herbal pantry. This is a simple procedure and very helpful for those starting to understand each herb's magical properties.

By coding your herb bottles and packets, you will not only remember what each one is for but also forever have easy access to your magical ingredients. Every time you open the pantry or cupboard, the color dots on the bottles and packets will let you know which herb to use to manifest your intention.

First, use the information in "Color Meaning" to make a list of the color tabs you will need. Take a quick trip to your grocery store's stationery section and look for color tabs or dots. They usually come in a sheet or in a box where you can pull out the dots. Don't worry if you think you'll never use them all, you will over time.

When you get home, use the list below and stick a color dot or tab to the corresponding herb or anything else in the pantry you wish to use as a magical ingredient. The chart at the end of the chapter lists magical intentions and their corresponding colors.

You may end up with two or three different colored tabs for each bottle, which will correspond to a magical need. Remember, some herbs have the same magical essence and over time you will need to exercise your own judgment as to which one works best for you. This is all trial and error, but the most important thing is to have fun with it! Enjoy the magic by knowing your herb pantry is ready for action at a moment's notice.

Allspice
Healing: White
Money: Green

Basil
Love: Pink
Protection: Black
Money: Green

Bay Leaves (Laurel)
Purification: Purple
Strength: Red
Protection: Black or Blue

Caraway
Protection: Black
Health: White or Blue

Cardamom Pods
Love: Pink
Passion: Red

Cayenne Pepper
Protection: Black
Strength: Red

Chicory
Strength: Red

Chili
Bring out arguments: Red

Cinnamon (Ground and Sticks)

Love: Pink
Success: Orange
Attraction: Red
Fruition of Dreams: Blue
Luck: Yellow

Cloves (Whole)

Love: Pink
Protection: Black
Money: Green

Coriander

Peace: Blue
Protection: Black

Cumin

Protection: Black

Curry Powder
Protection: Black

Dill
Protection: Black
Money: Green

Fennel
Healing: White or Blue

Ginger (ground)
Health: White
Money: Green
Success: Green

Marjoram
Love: Pink

Mint
Travel: Yellow
Protection while traveling: Blue
Protection: Black
Money: Green

Nutmeg (Whole and Ground)
Abundance: Yellow and Green

Parsley
Money: Green

Pepper—Black, Brown, White (Also Peppercorns)
Repellent: Black and Red

Rosemary
Everything you can think of: All colors

Saffron

Psychic Powers: Lavender
Healing: White
Chronic illness: Purple

Sage

Protection: Black
Cleansing: Purple
Healing: White
Purifying: White and Purple

Star Anise

Luck: Orange
Healing Powers: Purple, Lavender, Indigo

Tarragon

Healing: White
Feminine: Pink

Thyme
Healing: White

Turmeric
Purification: Purple
Protection: Black

Color Magic

Magical Intention	*Color*
Attraction	Red
Cleansing	Purple
Feminine	Pink
Fruition of dreams	Blue
Healing	White or Purple
Healing Powers	Purple or Indigo
Health	White or Blue
Love	Pink
Luck	Orange or Yellow
Money	Green

Color Magic (ctd.)

Magical Intention	*Color*
Passion	Red
Peace	Blue
Protection	Black or Blue
Psychic	Purple or Lavender
Purificatio	Purple
Purifying	White or Purple
Repellent	Black or Red
Strength	Red
Success	Green or Orange
Travel	Yellow or Green

ALLOWING OUTSIDE INFLUENCES

You can not only use color, herbs, flowers, and miscellaneous items you never thought had any magical meanings, but you can also draw on other forces to enhance your intent.

This includes working on your magic during certain Lunar phases or on certain days of the week and using color at different times of the month or week, especially if you are working with candles. We do this to tap into the energies that surround us and use those energies as vessels to manifest our reality. Tapping into these energies is not as hard as it sounds, and it gives your intention that extra magical *oomph* that you can use no matter what you need or want.

The Moon and its Phases

Working with Lunar phases is beautiful. At times, I find myself counting the days until the next Full Moon so I can do magic, and while I'm counting, I'm already visualizing the intent I want to send out. By doing so, I visualize my intent to the Universe for days, sometimes weeks. I like to think that I'm halfway to my intent when the actual Full Moon makes its presence known.

The Moon governs our planting seasons, tides, and emotions. The Moon is our spiritual Goddess and to her we send our intent. I have always visualized her as the Earth's caretaker and the one who sits by the side of sick children. She listens to our sadness and our cries for help. The Moon is truly the only one who understands the pain we go through, and she brings comfort to our unanswered questions.

The Moon is the crone who watches over us, the mother who gives birth to all things around us, and the maiden who grants wishes if you believe in what she is capable of accomplishing. She lets us tap into her energies as many times as we care to do so and the good thing about it is that it is all free of charge.

The Moon is the only element in the sky that I know of that changes on a daily basis. The Moon influences the ocean tides, planting, and fertility. During a Full Moon, more crimes are committed, changing animal behavior has been observed, and sleep deprivation has been reported.

The Moon is auspicious and mysterious and a favorable asset to our magical needs in conjunction with natural energies to cause an effect. Let the Moon be your guide to fruition and utilize it to its fullest potential.

Full Moon

The Full Moon is bright and round; you can see in the dark without light and driving at night is a much more pleasant experience. This is when the Moon has its greatest potential. All magical workings can be done during the Full Moon, be they positive, banishing, or whatever your needs are.

Waning Moon

Between the Full Moon and the New Moon, the Moon is waning; it is starting to decrease in size. This is a good time to work against any type of negative forces, such as banishing unwanted energies or eliminating self-doubt, your noisy neighbor, or your nagging boss.

New Moon

The New Moon cannot be seen; it is hidden from us all but still there. This is a great time for visualizing a new relationship and the beginnings of new things, especially things we've always wanted that were previously out of reach. Use this Moon phase to create your wishes and for them to prosper.

Waxing Moon

Between the New Moon and the Full Moon, the Moon is waxing; it is starting to increase in size. As it grows to its full potential, so can you. This is a good time to work on enhancing your needs and wants such as health or wealth because as the Moon grows so do your needs.

Days of the Week and the Planets

I dearly love working with the days of the week; they give my spells and intentions that little extra get-up-and-go that I need to manifest them. Make the days of the week a part of your daily ritual, from applying makeup to dedicating a glass of water to spirit.

The days of the week work in conjunction with the planets. Each planet has its own personality according to ancient planetary charts. The planets are influenced by the days of the week in which they govern. The planets, the Moon, and the Sun generate their essence for health, money, and happiness. Harvesting their energy will get you quicker to the intent you wish to come to fruition.

If you want to do a home cleaning, look at the day of the week that is best suited to this task, and do it on that day. I take all my magical baths according to the days of the week to tap into the specific energy.

Write the meanings of the days of the week on your calendar. This way, you'll get used to which day of the week is good for what intent. Further enhance your needs if you use the day of the week's corresponding color.

Sunday/Sun/Yellow

Sunday is the money and healing day. Use this day for those who need a little bit of healing, not only from physical ailments but also from spiritual ones. Do your money-need spells or intentions on this day. Sunday is also a great day for growth and financial development.

Use this day to find the strength within to see the things you want without feeling shy or uncomfortable in telling someone all that you wish to accomplish.

Monday/Moon/White

Monday is the spiritual day of the week; the day of attainment and discovery. Tap into the universal forces such as your deities or spiritual guides and ask them to guide you and enlighten your future path. Use this day for psychic workings and meditation to communicate with spirit.

Use the Moon phases to enhance your banishing and acquisitions of the things that are important to you.

Tuesday/Mars/Red

Tuesday is the day of leadership, strength, and courage. This is the day when we can combat those nasty negative energies with force and conviction. Mars and its day make us strong and more capable within ourselves to fight for what we believe in, and to endure for the rest of the week. Don't be shy in harnessing this energy, which is out there for the taking, to find a new, more sure and poised individual. Having the strength to look into life and not be scared of what it has to offer is something we all wish to have, and knowing you have this planet and day behind you is reassuring.

Wednesday/Mercury/Purple

Wednesday is the study day, not only academically, but also to study the person you are, or are becoming, by communicating your needs to those around you. Use this day for all your communication endeavors, from declaring your love to someone, communicating with your boss when she or he has been unreasonable, or simply opening communications with your family. This is the day you confess your wrongdoings and accept their ramifications.

This is a great day for you to work on your family and its happiness. This is the day to ask your boss for a promotion or a raise. You can also be true to yourself and express all your frustrations to those around you.

Thursday/Jupiter/Blue

This day of the week helps us not to abandon personal goals and aspirations. This day cements our ideas on paper and aids legal matters. If documents need to be signed for a favorable outcome, this is the day to do it. This is a day to go to court and fight against the world with a clear head for a positive outcome. Choose Thursday for any business ventures that have been out of reach, such as signing a contract, family matters, divorces, or any type of personal settlements.

Thursdays are good not only for legal matters but also for personal goals and the acquisition of money and riches.

Friday/Venus/Pink

Love day is Friday, which is totally governed by Venus, the love Goddess. Work on your relationship to make it more solid and binding. Light a candle for those in spirit to give them love and light on their journey.

On Fridays, do love spells; doing attraction spells on this day will result in a more positive outcome. Use this day for self-love and discovery for you and your future. This is the day you mend things with loved ones, such as lovers or family members—with the brother, mother, or father who you hold a grudge against for some past happening you haven't been able to forgive.

Saturday/Saturn/Black

Saturday is the day to be rid of negative energy and a terrific day to combat dark forces and spirits. I love my magical workings on Saturdays because I know the strength in my magic doubles, and I use this to my advantage.

Make this day your "banish" day. Use your mop and buckets with your banishing essences or herbs to clean the house from negativity, while leaving positive energy in your path.

If you want to get rid of something in your life, this is the day to do it. Get rid of the negativity that is not letting you move forward to the next stage of your life or preventing you from making decisions because of your lack of positivity.

38

BLENDING ENERGIES

There is a way to mix and blend energies together to cause a needed effect, and this is called the art of spell casting. Billions around the world unknowingly exercise some sort of spell through prayer. It doesn't matter your faith, religion, or cultural background, a prayer is just a positive visualization to communicate with spirits or a deity for health, money, well-being, or wishing relatives, family, and friends health and happiness.

We witches like to add a little bit of this herb or a little drop of that essential oil to communicate with spirit to change our circumstances for a favorable outcome by conducting a ritual known as a spell. I divide a spell into three categories:

Spell: The art of visualizing your needs to the Universe using words or chants and summoning universal forces or spirit to aid you with your intent.

Tools: Herbs, essences, color, Moon phases, days of the week, your athame, goblet, candles, or crystals. As you gather these tools for your spell, you're already focusing on your intent.

Rituals: The strength behind your intent. This is when you send it all to the Universe with feeling and belief, such as verbalizing, lighting candles, or simply focusing on all the above in a meditative state.

When you work with magic, it can take you back to a time when magic was very much tolerated and sought out by people, mainly for the manipulation of others. But humans have surpassed all that negativity and have evolved to a much gentler and less hateful society for the most part. We are more concerned with our own spiritual advancement and use magic mostly for our betterment.

There is one thing about spells; they are fun to put together. Spells are old as time and exciting to do, and their outcome is a mystery until they unfold. But let me assure you, they are easy to put together when you match energies with the intent you want to manifest.

When blending energies, make sure you have the right tools for your spell. If you are doing a love spell, you can't use healing herbs unless the spell requires healing love. If you are doing a spell for money, you don't want to do it on a Tuesday using red candles, but on a Thursday or a Sunday when the money energy is at its peak using green candles.

The list below includes intentions and the tools needed for that intention. Use this as a quick guide until you are comfortable using the items in your pantry and household to put energies together to cause an effect.

Happiness
....

Vegetable: Ginger

Flower: Gerberas

Fruit: Pineapple

Herb: Nutmeg

Essential oil: Bergamot

Color: Yellow

Planets: Mercury and the Sun

Days of the week: Wednesday and Sunday

Health
....

Vegetable: Lemongrass

Flower: Lavender

Fruit: Apple

Herb: Fennel

Essential oil: Fennel or Thyme

Color: White

Planet: Sun

Day of the Week: Sunday

Love
....

Vegetable: Leeks
Flower: Orchids
Fruit: Pear
Herb: Basil
Essential oil: Jasmine
Color: Pink
Planet: Venus
Day of the week: Friday

Money
....

Vegetable: Alfalfa
Flower: Roses (Red)
Fruit: Grapes
Herb: Basil
Essential oils: Cinnamon, Nutmeg, and Clove
Color: Green
Planets: Sun and Jupiter
Days of the week: Sunday and Thursday

Protection

. . . .

Vegetable: Artichoke

Flower: African Violet

Fruit: Blackberry

Herb: Sage (and Banishing)

Essential oils: Coriander, Basil, Dill, and Rosemary

Color: Black or Blue

Planets: Saturn and Moon

Days of the week: Saturday and Monday

CLEANSING YOUR HOME PHYSICALLY AND SPIRITUALLY

You know your home needs a little bit of sprucing up when, no matter how much you clean, it still feels dirty. The dirt you are feeling is not your everyday dirt. That dirt comes from negativity that has crept into your home without you knowing, making you feel unsettled in a place that is supposed to be your refuge. Then there are the times when you get an overwhelming feeling of crowdedness and sense everything is on top of you to the point where you want to move or throw stuff out. You move all sorts of things and furniture around in the hope of making you feel better, but after a few days, that feeling comes back again.

This is when you need to take action. These feelings are telling you that it is time to get rid of negative energies and make room for exciting new things, not only emotionally but also with material items.

Physical Cleansing

When you physically clean your home, I'm not suggesting you get rid of an old family heirloom or your grandmother's favorite china. I mean items that take up space with no meaning, use, or reason to be in your home. Take mugs, for example. These seem to accumulate rapidly when I really only need one set.

Look around your home for items you can get rid of, either by throwing them out or donating them. By doing this exercise, you tell yourself that it is all right to let go of emotional baggage. This is the key to moving emotionally forward in life and to let new things in, not only material but spiritual.

Cleaning your home is all about creating a positive space, one that you can be proud to be in. My mother-in-law used to say, "If you haven't used it for a year, the chances you'll use it the next are slim." Apply this saying to clothes and to anything else in your home, especially if there is no emotional attachment from you or your family.

Look in your sock drawer. This is crucial for those looking for love or a business partner. Make sure all your socks are in pairs. Get rid of anything else that is missing its pair or that is broken.

Once you've rid your home of all that you don't need or want, you'll feel a sense of lightness that comes from order and living in a friendly space without clutter. Once you have completed your sprucing-up, it is time for cleansing the home of negative energies to cement and ground your space.

Spiritual Cleansing

Cleanse your home on Saturdays, as this is the day to get rid of negative energies. Gather the following items on the kitchen counter: sage, a small fireproof container, matches, a white candle, a bowl filled with spring water, and a bowl filled with rock salt. As you gather these items, begin to think about the energy you want to banish and the energy you want to leave behind.

Begin by opening all your doors and windows. Place your hands over the items and meditate on why you are cleansing your home and what you wish to accomplish.

Place the sage in the fireproof container and light it. Light the candle. Pick up the bowl of water. Walk through your home and sprinkle the water in each room. As you do, say over and over, "*Element of Water, wash away negativity from my home.*"

Once finished, take the bowl back to the kitchen. Light the sage again if it has gone out. Pick up the bowl of salt. Walk through your home and sprinkle the salt in each room. As you do, say over and over, "*Element of Earth, strip away negativity from my home.*"

Once finished, take the bowl back to the kitchen. Light the sage again if it has gone out. Hold the candle with both hands and, thinking of the negativity you would like to burn while keeping it consistent with your intent, take the candle all through your home. As you do, say over and over, "*Element of Fire, burn away negativity from my home.*"

Once finished, take the candle back to the kitchen. Light the sage again if it has gone out. Pick up the container with the smoking sage and, in an anticlockwise direction, take the smoke all through your home. As you do, say over and over, "*Element of Air, take away from my home the negativity which it now holds.*" Once finished, take the sage back to the kitchen. Leave the candle lit and the sage burning, and close all your windows and doors. The next morning, vacuum away the salt.

Your home is now filled with positive spiritual abundance and is a clean living space. Do this cleansing every week, once a month, or whenever you feel it is time to re-cleanse.

REFLECTIONS IN CLOSING

One of the most important paths we will ever take is the path of self-discovery. This path can take us to places within ourselves we really didn't want to visit. This path is one of the most profound exposures we will ever encounter. With it comes the realization that self-criticism is the worst spell you can ever conjure. So treat your thoughts well and they will be positive companions, and let magic be a part of your life.

Magic is there for the taking when we learn to trust in something that offers no explanations. Magic gives us hope even if we don't feel or see its presence, but it is there, hidden in the shadows ready to be harnessed to its full potential using our own thoughts, wishes, and needed intent. Take what you have read in this book, learn from it, and apply it to your own life to cause a positive outcome to change your circumstances, bring love, seek protection, enhance finances, bring in happiness, and turn your life around.

Harness the magic within and around you and let the light of all there is in your heart. Believe in miracles because they do manifest and with a little aid from a herb, a safety pin, or a trivial nut to enhance your needs, you can never go wrong.

Blessings.

INDEX

Abundance, 78, 85, 150, 211, 328, 354

Achievement, 182

Affection, 312

African violet, 183, 348

Aggressive, 308

Air Element, 134, 277, 316, 353

Alchemic, 35

Alcohol, 76, 176

Alcohol dependency, 76

Alfalfa, 36, 37, 347

Allspice, 138, 200, 324

Alluring, 105, 218

Almond, 70, 76, 100, 118

Almond Flavor, 100

Almond Oil, 118

Amaryllis, 184

Ammonia, liquid, 257

Anise, 155, 163, 329

Anthurium, 184

Aphrodisiac, 95, 160, 199

Apple, 52, 53, 320, 346

Apricot, 53

Arguments, 143, 195, 325

Aspirations, 266, 277, 341

Athena, 115

Attract, 36, 43, 53, 54, 58, 78, 79, 96, 102, 105,
106, 108, 109, 118, 141, 144, 148, 149, 172, 203,
204, 208, 214, 218, 230, 279, 288, 312, 319, 320

Attraction, 96, 102, 105, 108, 140, 144, 163, 202,
203, 208, 230, 231, 301, 307, 326, 330, 341

Attractive, 54, 144, 233

Authority, 308

Avocado, 54, 118, 119

Avocado Oil, 118, 119

Baby Pins, 283

Baby Powder, 284

Baking, 36, 66, 99–103, 105–106, 317

Balloons, 284, 285

Bamboo, 185

Bananas, 54

Band-Aids, 285

Banishing, 14, 129, 161, 164, 198, 206, 214,
    222, 226, 229, 285, 294, 336, 339, 342, 348

Baptisms, 116

Barley, 8, 86

Basil, 5, 26, 133, 139, 140, 200, 263, 319, 320, 324, 347, 348

Bath, 43, 53, 56, 60, 62, 71, 72, 117–119, 121, 122, 124, 129, 130, 134, 140, 143, 147, 153, 156, 167, 169, 171–173, 186, 193, 198, 200–210, 212, 215, 218, 248, 253, 255, 258, 287, 300, 318, 319, 321, 322

Bathroom, 198, 260, 300

Bathtub, 109, 198, 274

Bay Leaves, 140, 324

Beauty, 18, 54, 72, 118, 179, 191, 229, 230, 232–234, 253

Bedpost, 260

Beer, 175, 176

Bees, 107

Bergamot, 71, 201, 221, 346

Bird of Paradise, 185

Birds, 66, 277–279

Black, 37, 58, 78, 80, 81, 83, 88, 130, 139, 141, 152, 161, 163, 237, 267, 284, 285, 288, 297, 305, 308, 309, 315, 318, 324–331, 342, 348

Black Salt, 130

Black Tea, 163

Blackberry, 55, 348

Bleach, 112, 256, 258, 260, 268

Blend, 37, 62, 111, 131, 199, 208, 212, 221, 242, 247–249, 251, 288, 292, 317–320, 343

Blessings, 202, 215, 356

Blue, 39, 41, 55, 56, 185, 189, 237, 261, 267, 268, 283, 295, 305, 306, 309, 310, 317, 318, 320, 324–328, 330, 331, 341, 348

Blue Ribbon, 56

Bluebird, 278

Blush, 193, 231, 236

Bodywash, 220, 221

Bolts, 269, 270

Bottles, 220, 242, 252, 317, 321–323

Brain, 19, 102, 295, 313

Brazil Nut, 77

Bread, 8, 65, 66, 69, 85, 103, 106, 175

Break, 56, 83, 168, 189, 190, 245, 257, 265, 266, 309

Breastfeeding, 38

Broom, 14, 260–262

Buckwheat, 86

Building, 267, 268, 295

Buns, 65

Burns, 108

Business, 9, 51, 76, 125, 139, 202, 206, 211, 308, 310, 341, 351

Buttons, 281, 286

Cake, 99–102

Calla Lily, 186

Calming, 183, 187, 190, 209, 215, 318

Candle, 39, 145, 287–289, 341, 352–354

Car, 89, 146, 266, 293, 305

Caraway, 141, 325

Carnation, 186

Carpet, 16, 262, 266

Carrier Oil, 215

Carrot, 39, 101

Cashew, 77

Cassia, 201

Cauliflower, 39

Cayenne Pepper, 142, 325

Cedar, 202

Celebration, 66

Celery, 40

Centerpiece, 41, 82, 120, 194

Chai, 163

Chakras, 27, 117, 306

Chamomile, 163, 202, 203, 221

Cheeks, 231

Cheese, 68

Cherry, 55, 56

Chestnut, 78

Chia Seeds, 78

Chicory, 142, 143, 325

Children, 166, 209, 214, 215, 258, 262, 284, 285, 306, 310, 313, 316, 334

Chili, 40, 143, 325

Chili Pepper, 40

Chocolate, 102

Christian, 116

Chrysanthemum, 187

Cinnamon, 53, 77, 102, 144, 145, 201, 203, 320, 326, 347

Citrine, 82

Citrus, 60, 288

Clarity, 22, 83, 94, 245

Clary Sage, 204

Cleanse, 14, 56, 72, 113, 128, 131, 132, 137, 153, 154, 168, 205, 211, 214, 220, 255, 262, 352

Cleansing, 30, 72, 92, 128, 129, 134, 154, 171, 172, 202, 206, 243, 257, 267, 291, 329, 330, 349, 350, 352, 354

Clearing, 58, 129, 209, 210, 221

Clove, 145, 204, 347

Coals, 137, 138, 140, 143, 145, 147, 149, 151, 153

Coconut, 56, 103, 119, 120, 172, 223

Coconut Oil, 119, 120

Coffee, 111, 159–162

Coffee grounds, 161

Colds, 155, 263

Color, 51, 103, 104, 136, 231, 232, 237, 238, 242, 251, 252, 285, 288, 305, 307–317, 320–323, 330, 331, 333, 338, 344, 346–348

Comb, 233, 234

Comforting, 201, 223

Commitment, 283

Communication, 224, 225, 312, 319, 340

Compost, 48

Concentration, 40, 199

Conception, 39, 81, 124, 188, 201, 213, 311

Conditioner, 222, 233

Confidence, 225, 230, 234, 235, 308

Conglomerate, 229

Conquest, 142

Coriander, 143, 326, 348

Corn, 41, 120, 226

Corn Oil, 120

Cotton, 37, 43, 207, 213, 223, 224, 251, 261, 295, 296

Cotton Balls, 213, 223, 224, 296

Cotton Wool, 295

Courage, 58, 75, 141, 164, 235, 309, 314, 321, 339

Cramping, 39

Cranberry, 57

Creative, 113, 277, 313, 322

Crow, 278

Cultures, 14, 47, 67, 86, 127, 128, 134, 243, 260

Current, 189

Cypress, 204, 205

Daffodil, 187

Dandelion, 163

Death, 308

Deity, 18, 315, 319, 343

Depression, 308, 314

Dill, 146, 147, 327, 348

Dirt, 15, 16, 45, 128, 248, 250, 255, 262, 306, 349

Dirty, 169, 250, 349

Disappear, 285

Divination, 55, 216

Divine, 219, 320

Doorframe, 260

Dreams, 28, 36, 43, 53, 66, 68, 122, 128, 144, 203, 211–213, 247, 251, 266, 277, 293, 312–314, 316, 326, 330

Eagle, 278

Earl Grey, 163

Earth, 4, 48, 83, 246, 334

Earth Element, 14, 129, 247, 353

Echinacea, 163

Elements, 244

Encouragement, 311, 312, 319, 320

Energy, 3, 14, 15, 27, 28, 30, 36, 59, 60, 71, 72, 75,
79, 92, 108, 112, 117, 119, 124, 128, 130, 134,
137, 138, 140, 149, 153, 156, 160, 182, 186, 188,
189, 191, 194, 199, 205, 206, 209, 210, 212, 222,
244, 246, 247, 255, 260, 262, 266, 267, 275, 278,
298, 300, 306, 307, 315, 321, 338, 340, 342, 345, 352

Epsom salt, 130

Essence, 3, 18, 36, 51, 52, 71–73, 91, 131, 133,
134, 136, 139, 145, 151, 153, 181, 182, 186–188,
191–193, 197, 198, 200, 203, 211, 212, 234,
238, 247, 256, 260, 283, 287, 298, 312, 323, 338

Eucalyptus, 163, 199, 205, 263

Exfoliate, 72

Eye Shadow, 231, 232, 237

Eyeliner, 235

Feminine, 39, 45, 71, 156, 192,
215, 229, 230, 312, 329, 330

Fennel, 147, 205, 263, 296, 327, 346

Fertility, 39, 57, 75, 89, 92, 101,
   117, 187, 201, 213, 273, 335

Fig, 57

Finances, 4, 37, 58, 108, 146, 147, 149, 151, 256, 319, 356

Financial Stability, 26, 36, 46, 66, 68, 89

Fire Element, 14, 353

Flowers, 5, 14, 40, 47, 58, 124, 135, 181–183, 185–
   187, 189, 190, 192–194, 253, 274, 275, 333

Food Coloring, 104, 317–322

Food Storage Container, 290

Forgiveness, 187

Fork, 243, 244, 251

Fossils, 242

Foundation, 232, 233

Frankincense, 206

Fresh, 5, 17, 25, 36, 37, 41, 43, 51, 55, 56, 58, 65, 134, 135, 139, 143, 146–149, 151–154, 156, 167, 172, 207, 209, 212, 225, 252, 271, 274, 295, 296, 319, 321

Friday, 320, 341, 347

Friendships, 103, 312

Fruit, 51, 52, 55, 56, 60–62, 173, 307, 346–348

Fun, 4, 27, 105, 155, 255, 284, 293, 317, 324, 345

Garden, 48, 133, 134, 183, 188–190, 244, 274, 275

Gardenia, 188

Garlic, 42

Gentle, 67, 71, 73, 111, 112, 169, 192, 200, 201, 209, 223, 224, 282, 284, 300, 312

Geranium, 207

Gerbera, 189

Gift, 51, 134, 193, 274, 283, 286

Ginger, 43, 104, 148, 163, 207, 327, 346

Glass, 8, 68, 72, 79, 83, 96, 106, 121, 168, 169, 176, 242, 244, 245, 249, 266, 318, 322, 337

Goal, 22, 282, 316

God, 13, 75, 177, 269, 282

Goddess, 13, 52, 72, 73, 115, 177, 182, 205, 230, 247, 282, 315, 334, 341

Gossip, 80, 138

Grains, 7, 8, 66, 85, 87

Grape Seed Oil, 120, 121

Grapes, 58, 347

Gratitude, 99

Green, 36–38, 40, 41, 43–45, 47, 48, 52–54, 58, 59, 61, 80, 81, 86, 105, 115, 118, 120, 133, 139, 145, 148, 163, 185, 237, 293, 305, 306, 310, 311, 319, 324, 326–328, 330, 331, 345, 347

Green Beans, 43

Green Tea, 163

Grocery, 7, 25, 52, 75, 119, 127, 135–137, 160, 166, 171, 175, 182, 183, 188, 191, 199, 239, 243, 265, 275, 281, 284, 286, 317, 323

Grounding, 79, 128, 129, 195, 263

Hair, 129, 222, 223, 233, 234, 237, 239, 291

Hairbrush, 18, 233

Hammer, 83, 267, 268

Handbag, 150, 234

Hangover, 76

Happiness, 3–5, 14, 35, 36, 43, 48, 60, 62, 65, 66, 94, 102, 155, 158, 171, 173, 176, 186, 193, 201, 212, 220, 237, 249, 252, 255, 270, 275, 278, 282, 288–290, 297, 299, 307, 311, 312, 316, 338, 340, 343, 346, 356

Happy, 47, 58, 62, 135, 151, 173, 186, 187, 189, 207, 210, 212, 305, 310, 312

Hardware, 18, 265

Harvest, 66

Hazelnuts, 79, 121

Headaches, 45

Healing, 52, 87, 108, 115, 134, 138, 147, 153–157,
    169, 186, 190, 194, 200, 202, 204, 205, 217,
    223, 224, 245, 250, 263, 277, 285, 296, 307,
    309, 311, 315, 318, 324, 327, 329, 330, 338, 345

Health, 4, 5, 10, 14, 35, 37, 43, 52, 70, 75, 87, 89,
    94, 100, 104, 123, 125, 130, 141, 143, 148,
    153, 155, 156, 163, 164, 177, 204, 207, 214,
    215, 231, 233, 255, 256, 259, 274, 282, 290,
    298, 318, 325, 327, 330, 337, 338, 343, 346

Herbalism, 36, 133

Herbs, 3, 7, 14, 102, 133–137, 152, 154, 177, 247, 248,
    252, 263, 275, 290, 318, 322, 323, 333, 342, 344, 34

Hex, 44, 190

Himalayan Salt, 131

Home, 3, 5, 14–16, 22, 28, 30, 31, 37, 40–42, 44, 47, 52–55, 58–60, 62, 65, 66, 72, 77, 79, 80, 86–89, 93, 102, 103, 111–113, 116, 120, 127–130, 136, 138–143, 150, 151, 154, 155, 158, 165, 166, 168, 169, 172, 175, 177, 182, 183, 185–189, 191–195, 201, 202, 204–207, 209, 211, 212, 214–217, 225, 232, 233, 244, 253, 255, 257–260, 262, 263, 265–268, 270, 279, 281, 286, 287, 291, 292, 294, 297–300, 305, 309, 312, 313, 316, 318, 323, 338, 349–354

Honey, 65, 104, 107–109

Honeybush, 109, 163

Horseradish, 44

House, 15, 47, 54, 60, 65, 87, 91, 96, 97, 105, 128, 137, 151–155, 185, 200, 234, 260, 261, 293, 319, 342

Hungry, 47, 71, 86

Hydrangea, 189

Hydrogen Peroxide, 291

Hygiene, 18, 25, 179, 199, 219, 220, 226

Ice Cream, 69, 70

Illnesses, 148, 313, 318

Imagination, 19, 153, 313

Indigo, 313, 329, 330

Injuries, 147, 205

Injustice, 309, 315

Interview, 144, 154, 203

Intuitive, 210, 216, 256, 313

Intuitiveness, 210, 320

Jars, 152, 220, 274, 292

Jasmine, 163, 203, 208, 263, 347

Jealous, 233, 236, 259, 310

Jewelry, 59, 131, 299

Job, 80, 144, 154, 203, 208, 221, 298

Jojoba Oil, 208

Journey, 36, 70, 154, 155, 245, 309, 341

Jupiter, 341, 347

Justice, 315

Karma, 313, 316

Kindness, 187

Kitchen, 42, 77, 116, 157, 206, 244, 249, 260, 352–354

Knife, 246, 247, 251

Lammas, 66

Laurel, 140, 324

Lavender Color, 313, 329, 331

Lavender Oil, 71, 199, 209, 224, 263, 320

Lavender Plant, 177, 190, 346

Leaves, 38, 44, 45, 47, 58, 117, 140, 149,
    150, 153–155, 172, 295, 318, 320, 324

Leek, 44

Legumes, 8, 66, 85, 89

Lemon, 58, 59, 163, 209, 221

Lemongrass, 148, 163, 210, 346

Lettuce, 45

Licorice, 163

Lightbulb, 268

Lily, 186, 190

Lime, 59, 223

Linden, 164

Lipstick, 18, 234–236

Loaf, 65

Longevity, 58, 73, 163, 186, 204, 209

Lore, 47, 52

Love, 3–5, 14, 28, 35, 37, 38, 44, 48, 52–56, 61, 62, 77, 78, 96, 100, 102–106, 112, 116, 118, 135, 136, 139–142, 144, 145, 148, 149, 156–158, 163, 169, 176, 184, 187, 188, 190–193, 198, 200, 203–205, 207–209, 211, 213, 216, 217, 221, 223, 231, 232, 237, 249, 252, 255, 263, 270–272, 275, 277, 282, 284, 287–290, 295–297, 307, 309, 311–313, 320, 324–327, 330, 337, 340–342, 345, 347, 351, 356

Luck, 52, 53, 62, 75, 79, 121, 155, 163, 185, 223, 310, 326, 329, 330

Lust, 61, 148, 163, 314

Macadamia, 79, 122

Macadamia Oil, 122

Magazine, 292

Magical, 1, 3–5, 13, 15, 17–19, 22, 26–31, 36, 42, 51, 52, 60–62, 69, 71, 72, 75, 76, 91, 92, 95, 102, 107, 108, 115, 117–119, 121, 124, 128–130, 133–136, 138–140, 150–154, 156, 161, 162, 167, 168, 171, 175, 177, 181, 182, 200, 205, 206, 210, 211, 213, 215, 216, 218, 224, 230, 241–243, 246–248, 252, 253, 255, 257, 258, 261, 267, 268, 271, 273, 274, 277, 281, 282, 289, 290, 292, 296, 300, 301, 303, 307, 309, 311, 315, 317, 318, 322, 323, 330, 331, 333–336, 338, 342

Magpie, 278

Makeup, 223, 229, 230, 232, 235–237, 337

Makeup Remover, 236

Marjoram, 149, 327

Mars, 339

Mascara, 237

Masculine, 75, 79, 202

Matches, 220, 294, 352

Mattress, 141, 148

Mead, 107

Medicinal, 133

Mental Stability, 313

Mercury, 340, 346

Milk, 56, 67, 70–73, 160, 172, 175

Millet, 87

Mind, 13, 19–22, 26, 27, 29, 30, 60, 94, 100,
    121, 125, 128, 139, 154, 164, 169, 202, 216,
    220, 248, 261, 275, 282, 301, 307, 309, 313, 316

Mint, 133, 149, 150, 164, 224, 328

Miscellaneous Items, 281–301, 333

Misery, 69, 308

Monday, 339, 348

Money, 3, 36, 43, 58, 82, 86, 88, 104–106, 109,
    120, 122, 123, 138–140, 144–151, 153, 163,
    164, 176, 200, 202, 204, 207, 208, 211, 224,
    225, 237, 252, 263, 288, 290, 307, 310, 319,
    324, 326–328, 330, 338, 341, 343, 345, 347

Mood, 102, 306, 307

Moon, 42, 71, 242, 252, 306, 334–339, 344, 348

Mop, 169, 172, 200, 205, 211, 214, 217, 260, 262, 263, 342

Mortar and Pestle, 37, 48, 247

Motivating, 212

Mouthwash, 224, 225

Myrrh, 210

Nail Polish, 237, 238

Nail Polish Remover, 237, 238

Nails, 145, 237, 238, 267, 268

Needle and Thread, 295, 298

Negative, 15, 16, 18, 30, 36, 40, 56, 59, 60, 71,
72, 92, 112, 119, 124, 128, 130, 134, 140, 152,
153, 189, 205, 206, 210, 220, 222, 223, 233,
238, 246, 249, 255–257, 260–262, 266–268,
292, 294, 308, 315, 336, 339, 342, 350, 352

Negotiating, 308

Neptune, 243

Nettle, 164

Newspaper, 292

Nutmeg, 150, 211, 212, 328, 346, 347

Nuts, 75, 77, 79, 80, 269

Oats, 8, 87, 88

Occult, 278

Offerings, 18, 51, 107, 177

Oil, 115–124, 152, 176, 197–218, 224, 253, 289, 295, 299, 300, 320, 343, 346, 347

Olive Branches, 116

Olive Oil, 115–117, 289

Onion, 46

Orange, 39, 40, 53, 60–62, 81, 87, 101, 123, 124, 173, 185, 189, 193, 194, 212, 213, 291, 311, 312, 319, 320, 326, 329–331

Orchid, 191

Pacification, 96

Padlock, 270

Pain, 48, 93, 159, 194, 201, 282, 283, 314, 335

Paper, 9, 37, 41, 44, 45, 48, 53, 66, 78, 81, 88, 96, 100, 105, 109, 139, 143, 148, 152, 160, 161, 168, 190, 224, 226, 243, 245, 249, 251, 268, 284, 292, 293, 296, 297, 318, 319, 341

Parsley, 47, 151, 328

Passion Flower, 164

Pastry, 99

Patchouli, 213

Peace, 52, 53, 71, 80, 99, 117, 137, 143, 144, 157, 163, 164, 169, 184, 193, 202, 204, 224, 249, 263, 275, 277, 287, 309, 312, 315, 318, 326, 331

Peach, 61

Pear, 61, 347

Pecan, 80

Pen, 80, 296, 297

Pentacle, 260

Peony, 192

Pepper, 40, 142, 152, 325, 328

Peppercorn, 152

Peppermint, 164, 213

Perception, 233, 278, 316

Perfume, 181

Persistence, 316

Pesticides, 8, 136

Petals, 45, 149, 186, 191, 193–195, 271

Pillow, 43, 54, 87, 144, 145, 148, 156, 157, 190, 203, 207, 212, 213, 217, 250, 296

Pin, 3, 283, 298, 307, 356

Pineapple, 62, 173, 346

Pink, 37–39, 45, 54, 78, 105, 131, 184, 193, 242, 271, 283, 306, 310, 312, 320, 324–327, 329, 330, 341, 347

Pink Ribbon, 38, 45

Pistachio nut, 80

Plates, 248, 266

Plumbing, 58

Poppy Seeds, 81

Positive, 4, 15, 18, 21, 22, 30, 36, 58, 69, 70, 108, 123, 137, 157, 162, 172, 173, 198, 203, 217, 219, 239, 244, 246, 259, 266, 282, 293, 297, 315, 317, 336, 341–343, 351, 354–356

Potato, 47, 48

Pots, 152, 183, 188, 248, 274

Power, 10, 21, 27, 61, 82, 134, 143,
144, 206, 208, 295, 308, 311, 314

Preserving, 8

Produce, 3, 17, 25, 27, 31, 35, 274

Property, 96, 97, 117, 203, 211

Prosperity, 3, 52, 54, 63, 65, 66, 68, 77,
85, 87–89, 101, 121, 122, 293, 310

Protection, 4, 5, 14, 35, 37, 40, 42, 43, 46, 52, 55, 56,
59, 75, 76, 83, 86, 88, 89, 100, 103, 115, 118, 119,
122, 124, 139–143, 145–149, 153, 154, 157,
163, 183, 185, 193, 200, 204–207, 210, 224,
229, 233, 238, 249, 257, 258, 282, 285, 294,
298, 307, 309, 315, 318, 324–331, 348, 356

Psychic, 153, 204, 206, 210, 216,
313, 316, 320, 329, 331, 339

Psychic Work, 204, 210

Pumpkin Seeds, 81

Purification, 47, 70–72, 140, 151, 157, 164, 324, 330

Purity, 72, 193, 248, 315

Purple, 39, 42, 46, 47, 58, 80, 183, 185, 190,
    193, 306, 313, 320, 321, 324, 329–331, 340

Purse, 86, 109, 148–151, 155, 207, 238, 320

Razors, 229, 239

Reading, 29, 40, 206

Red, 37, 40, 42, 45–47, 52, 55, 57, 58, 62, 63, 82,
    88, 137, 142, 143, 148, 177, 184, 189, 193,
    213, 235, 261, 288, 294, 301, 305, 306, 314, 317,
    319–321, 324–326, 328, 330, 331, 339, 345, 347

Red Jasper, 82

Reflective, 162, 166

Regenerating, 47

Reiki, 154

Relax, 72, 123, 143, 177, 199, 201, 202, 208, 287

Relaxing, 72, 177, 199, 208

Renewal, 73, 94, 190

Repellent, 152, 210, 328, 331

Resins, 3, 137, 181, 247

Ribbons, 14, 42

Rice, 70, 88, 122

Rice Bran Oil, 122

Riches, 68, 77, 341

Road, 130, 146

Rock Salt, 131, 352

Romantic, 177, 191, 208, 225, 251

Rooibos Tea, 164

Rope, 270, 271

Rose, 45, 123, 149, 164, 192, 208, 215, 216, 271, 295

Rose Hip, 123, 164

Rose Hip Oil, 123

Rosemary, 133, 152, 153, 214, 223, 263, 295, 318, 328, 348

Runes, 206

Sad, 173, 193, 305

Safeguard, 76, 80

Safety Pin, 3, 298, 307, 356

Saffron, 153, 154, 329

Sage, 154, 155, 164, 204, 329, 348, 352–354

Salt, 8, 16, 127–132, 167, 168, 261–263, 352–354

Sandalwood, 208, 216

Sarsaparilla, 164

Saturday, 258, 342, 348

Saturn, 342, 348

Scissors, 249

Sea Salt, 132

Seal, 72, 262, 267

Sedative, 308

Sesame Seeds, 82

Sexual Intercourse, 188

Shampoo, 222, 233

Sheets, 201, 250, 251

Shoelaces, 298

Shoes, 146, 151, 298, 299

Shopping, 3–5, 7, 10, 25–28, 116

Sickness, 147, 177, 205, 263

Skin, 72, 108, 109, 117–119, 124, 129, 130, 134,
     208, 229, 231, 233, 236, 239, 250, 258, 271

Sleep, 54, 93, 164, 190, 199, 203, 209, 250, 255, 313, 335

Smell, 60, 65, 147, 162, 181, 190, 205, 214, 219, 247, 257

Socks, 266, 281, 299, 351

Sodium Chloride, 127

Soothing, 187

Sorrow, 308

Space, 14–16, 52, 61, 128, 129, 138, 154, 157, 166, 198,
     206, 236, 255, 262, 274, 285, 300, 350–352, 354

Spearmint, 217, 320

Spell, 15, 30, 44, 144, 152, 153,
    168, 189, 314, 343–345, 355

Spell Breaker, 44, 189

Sperm Count, 39, 57

Spices, 15, 102, 133, 145, 275

Spirit, 14, 15, 26, 71, 133, 182, 187, 193, 194, 202,
    206, 207, 215, 245, 273, 277, 278, 287, 289,
    300, 312, 313, 315, 320, 337, 339, 341, 343, 344

Spiritual, 3, 4, 7, 14, 15, 35, 36, 62, 73, 92, 128, 129, 134,
    153, 154, 156, 169, 171–173, 186, 188, 190, 199, 200,
    204, 205, 208, 215–217, 220, 223, 232, 239, 245, 253,
    255, 259, 266, 268, 275, 283, 288, 291, 300, 306, 310–
    313, 315, 320, 321, 334, 338, 339, 345, 351, 352, 354

Spiritual Dirt, 255

Spiritual Energy, 3, 14, 188

Spirituality, 39, 73, 105, 188, 201, 216, 250, 307, 315

Spoon, 70, 251, 252

Sprinkles, 105, 292

Sprucing, 349

Stability, 3, 26, 31, 36, 46, 47, 66, 68, 89, 149, 151, 313

Stalks, 148

Star Anise, 155, 329

Strength, 46, 58, 60, 63, 79, 134, 140–142, 144,
    156, 162–164, 184, 190, 191, 193, 194, 212,
    215, 220, 262, 269, 270, 274, 287, 308, 314,
    321, 324, 325, 331, 339, 340, 342, 344

Stress, 19, 102, 199, 203, 218, 274, 313

Success, 43, 104, 144, 148, 203, 207, 326, 327, 331

Sugar, 95–97, 171, 292

Sun, 63, 105, 175, 222, 265, 269, 305, 338, 346, 347

Sunday, 58, 63, 87, 96, 139, 158, 209, 338, 345–347

Sunflower, 83, 124, 194

Sunflower Oil, 124

Sunflower Seeds, 83

Super Glue, 271

Supermarket, 3–5, 10, 17, 19, 25, 26, 29, 31, 135, 190, 220, 247, 257, 266, 299

Symbolism, 14

Tarot Cards, 206

Tarragon, 156, 329

Tea, 108, 109, 111, 155, 159, 160, 162, 163, 202, 299, 300

Tea Light, 299, 300

Thursday, 341, 345, 347

Thyme, 156, 157, 217, 296, 321, 330, 346

Tile, 266

Toilet Paper, 226

Tomato, 48, 63

Toothbrush, 224

Toothpaste, 224

Towels, 253

Tranquility, 309

Travel, 10, 62, 134, 149, 278, 328, 331

Trident, 243

Truth, 83, 309

Tuesday, 339, 345

Turmeric, 157, 158, 330

Understanding, 53, 69, 187, 194,
    217, 309, 310, 312, 315, 316

Underwear, 300, 301

Universe, 19, 21, 199, 219, 245,
    282, 283, 290, 293, 316, 334, 344

Urine, 226

Vacuum, 15, 16, 87, 128, 142, 354

Vampires, 259

Vanilla Extract, 101, 106

Vase, 5, 41, 79, 120, 121, 186, 193, 253

Vegetable, 35, 47, 346–348

Venus, 341, 347

Vinegar, 111–113, 256

Violet, 183, 313, 348

Vision Board, 293, 294

Visions, 164, 204, 213

Wallet, 58, 86, 108, 109, 140, 144,
    147–151, 153, 155, 207, 238

Walnut, 83, 124

Water, 14, 39, 42, 53, 72, 78, 85, 89, 96, 106, 107, 109, 112,
    113, 129, 130, 132, 134, 135, 139, 140, 158, 165–169,
    172, 198, 199, 221, 242–246, 248, 249, 252, 253, 258,
    260, 263, 278, 291, 292, 317–322, 337, 352, 353

Water Element, 14, 134, 166, 169, 221, 353

Wealth, 14, 37, 41, 100, 120, 163,
    176, 211, 249, 288, 298, 337

Wednesday, 96, 340, 346

Well-being, 4, 221, 257, 314, 343

White, 3, 39, 42–47, 62, 70, 71, 73, 78, 83, 87,
    88, 92, 94–96, 103, 111–113, 132, 150, 152,
    155–157, 169, 177, 186–188, 193, 198, 206,
    224, 237, 248, 250, 253, 260, 262, 271, 283, 288,
    296, 306, 315, 324, 325, 327–331, 339, 346, 352

White Spells, 3

Windowsill, 63, 260

Wine, 68, 175–177, 245

Wisdom, 3, 115, 162, 278

Wishes, 38, 61, 100, 128, 134, 163, 185,
    194, 203, 216, 277, 289, 335, 337, 355

Woodpecker, 278

Yeast, 106, 107, 176

Yellow, 40, 41, 46, 54, 58, 63, 101, 104, 115, 118, 120–
    125, 153, 157, 186, 193, 194, 269, 271, 305, 306,
    316, 317, 319, 322, 326, 328, 330, 331, 338, 346

Ylang-Ylang, 218

Yogurt, 73